# humor us

## AMERICA'S FUNNIEST HUMORISTS ON THE POWER OF LAUGHTER

Copyright © 2006 BMP Publications

Printed in the USA

Cover and Page Design by Connection Graphics

Published by:

Brad Montgomery, CSP

Brad Montgomery Productions

Denver, CO

800.624.4280


ISBN: 0-9743409-2-8

This book is sold with the understanding that the subject matter is of a general nature and does not constitute medical, legal, or other professional advice for any specific individual or situation. Readers planning to take action in any areas that this book describes should seek professional advice from their doctors, specialists, and other advisors, as would be prudent or advisable under their given circumstances. However if readers just plan to lighten up, take themselves a bit less seriously and maybe tell a knock-knock joke, we say, "Go for it."

Additional copies of *Humor Us* can be obtained through any of the authors in this book. Contact information follows each chapter and can be found again at the end of the book.

# Acknowledgments

This book is a great example of how many people working together can produce something better than someone working alone.

I am grateful to the other 17 authors in this book who are more than just funny people. They are mentors, speakers, performers and friends. I am more flattered and appreciative for their participation in *Humor Us* than they will ever guess.

Eric Chester, CSP is a wonderful speaker, author and publisher. I am enormously grateful for his help, advice, and generosity.

Thanks to Connie Sweet of Connection Graphics (www.connectiongraphics.com) for making this book look beautiful. To Anita Robeson, Sandy Guerra-Cline, and Lindsay Smith who helped us edit. Thanks especially to Kim Wooldridge for her expertise with the written word.

Finally, thank you to my family: Kim, Claire, Ben and Paige. They keep me grounded. They keep me guessing. And they keep me laughing.

— **Brad Montgomery**
**Publisher and Contributing Author**

# Humor Us:
# Table of Contents

# ☺ INTRODUCTION

## What is this book?

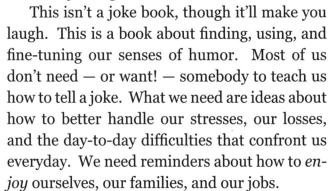

Here's an idea: Ask 18 of America's funniest motivational speakers, humorists and comedians to submit their best ideas about the Power of Laughter. Ask them to write on everything from Humor-and-Marriage to Humor-and-Business to Humor-and-Creativity. And then put those ideas in a book. What do you get? *Humor Us: America's Funniest Humorists on the Power of Laughter.*

This isn't a joke book, though it'll make you laugh. This is a book about finding, using, and fine-tuning our senses of humor. Most of us don't need — or want! — somebody to teach us how to tell a joke. What we need are ideas about how to better handle our stresses, our losses, and the day-to-day difficulties that confront us everyday. We need reminders about how to *enjoy* ourselves, our families, and our jobs.

This book is made up of chapters written by folks just like you. (Well, not exactly like you, unless you make your living on stage making folks laugh and delivering messages of hope, humor, and attitude.)

But like you, the authors are struggling to find their way in a complex and often not-so-funny world. They aren't counselors or PhDs, though each of those professions are represented here. They are normal people with abnormal jobs: they are humorists. They study humor for a living, and then use that knowledge to make people laugh and to convey a positive message. And now they're sharing that wisdom with you.

## What's Humor to You?

Humor doesn't mean you have to be a clown, play practical jokes, or even laugh out loud with your boss. (Though maybe you should do all of those things.) Humor is an *attitude*. Improving your sense of humor might mean as little as being less dour, less uptight, and less severe. Sure, it *might* mean that you laugh more each day. (And frankly, we hope you do.) But improving your sense of humor could be as simple as just being a bit more *glad*.

So sit back, pour yourself a cup of coffee, and get ready to lighten up. Our world is often serious and occasionally very difficult. That's all the more reason why we all need reminders about the Power of Laughter. Don't wait... Turn the page and get started now.

# Take Out Anything That's Not Funny

## ...the habit of champions!

**By Mike Rayburn**

## This is not about comedy.

As the last of the Sunday night crowd found the door, trading thick bar smoke for thin winter air, I turned anxiously to my friend Kier and asked, "So, what did you think?"

We were at Zanie's Comedy Showplace in Nashville, Tennessee. After playing more than a thousand shows at colleges, this was my first week headlining a comedy club.

I had invited Kier Irmiter, a fellow guitar-comic to come and critique my show. Though it can be ego bruising it's been said that feedback is the breakfast of champions ...and big money if you're the Sex Pistols (that's a guitar-player joke).

Anyway, I felt good about the show, but I also know that if you start believing all the wonderful things they say about you, your skills stop growing and your head makes up the difference (anyone remember Terrence Trent Darby?). So I waited for Kier's response.

## Remember, this is not about comedy

"Man, there's nothing specific I would change," he replied kindly, "but I have a general suggestion. Go home and script your entire show. Write down everything you say on stage — every story, lyric, set-up, punch line; every "yeah,' um,' etc."

"Then," and he said this with emphasis, "Take out anything that's not funny."

I laughed at that. He didn't. I thought about it. Then I got it. I'm a comedian. Laughs are what matters. So take out anything that's not funny. How simultaneously simple and profound!

Less is more, right? (Unless you're anorexic). I sometimes joke that I don't have a way with words, just a whole lot of them. If ten words say it well, I'll try to wow 'em with twenty. That's as wrong as thinking that if two pills will relieve your cold, then ten should cure it completely ... yeah, the same way cancer cures smoking.

# (We're getting there)

Anyway, I took Kier's advice, went home, scripted my show and started chopping. The result? In a 60-minute comedy set, I cut more than ten minutes worth of words, set-ups and parts of stories that were irrelevant and unnecessary. Unbelievable! Then I remembered reading that Jerry Seinfeld will spend an hour trying to reduce an eight-word joke to five. I figured that since Jerry has had, well, a little success, maybe there's something to this.

Something to this? Friends, something amazing happened the next time I walked on stage. Without all the needless stuff, my show took off! I had climbed aboard a rocket. The pace was faster, the audience reaction better, and the momentum caused me to tap into new creative areas just to keep up with myself. That one suggestion took my show, and thus my career, to a whole new level.

## I told you this is not about comedy

Do you see where we're going? A great sculptor was once asked how he carved such a beautiful bird from a chunk of marble. "I just took out anything that didn't look like a bird," he replied.

Well, yeah.

So what if as a salesperson you took out anything you're doing that isn't selling your product? What if as a business owner you took out anything that isn't helping your business? What if as a parent you took out anything you do that doesn't make for good parenting? What if as a spouse you took out anything you do, say or think that doesn't nurture your relationship? What if you examined your life and the way you spend your time and took out anything that isn't important? What if we all trim the useless fat out of our lives and take some "Slimfast for the Soul"? I believe our lives would rocket to levels unimagined!

## This is about everything

Since funny is what is relevant to a comedian, let's expand that phrase for everyone: "Take out anything that's not relevant."

This of course means we have to first develop the ability to discern what's funny or not, what's relevant or not. Josh Wainright, my manager, has a unique ability to find what's funny. He once shanked a golf shot so badly that it would take a miracle to recover. Low and behold, a miracle was in store, and his unbelievable follow-up put him nicely on the green. Josh's dad, shaking his head in amazement, said, "What was THAT?" Without missing a beat, Josh replied, "That was the Josh-Shank Redemption."

Find what's funny. Find what's relevant. Get rid of the rest.

## This is about me

I'm pretty much a cassette tape guy in an iPod world (and I suppose in ten years I'll be an iPod guy in a "new techno-thing" world). In an age of WiFi and broadband, I'm still impressed with color TV. As a guitarist, my favorite electronic effect is a pick. However, I *love* my laptop computer. Why? One reason: the delete key. (That and a shredder, and I could work for Arthur Andersen.) It's the best cure for my wordiness. Ask the editors: this chapter started off as a book. Make friends with your delete key, metaphorically and literally. Folks, the key to life is editing.

## This is about you ... and your Tupperware

Taking out anything that's not funny or relevant also means editing the physical "stuff" in our lives. We are a society with too much stuff (read: crap). We all need to clean out the garage. How many Garden Weasels, pieces of wood, bicycle tubes that need patching, trombones you saved from the third grade, chairs you're gonna fix, boxes of cards, graded papers, and old magazines do you need, exactly? Are you ever going to read those publications? Or worse, do you kid yourself that they'll "be worth something someday"? Unless you've got the Magna Carta in there, or the Jimi Hendrix set list that says "Foxy Lady, Purple Haze, set guitar on fire, worship ....," throw them away. They're neither relevant nor funny.

I recently found in my garage a plaster cast from when I broke my thumb in ninth grade. Apparently, at some point I thought, "Boy, my kids will really want to see this someday." It's like saving a kidney stone or videotaping childbirth . . . very classy. Nothing like sharing stuff removed from your body with a close friend. Or a movie of it being removed. Invite the neighbors! When I showed my wife the cast, she was dumbfounded. "You *saved* this?" And for a brief moment, I actually tried to justify it. Aah! Take it out!

Here's the kicker. Instead of editing our stuff, we try to store and stash. We buy stuff for our stuff. What is a paperweight? A piece of stuff to put on your stuff to make room for more stuff.

I bet you have a cabinet somewhere in your kitchen un-stackably crammed with Tupperware containers, all hope-lessly divorced from their tops. So it's now *dysfunctional* stuff for your stuff. And deep inside you have a subconscious avoidance of that cabinet, a fear of releasing the landslide, and God forbid having to match a bottom and a top. So, rather than organize them (impossible), you buy . . . Sa-ran Wrap, the universal, one-size-fits-all, Tupperware top. Which, of course, qualifies for more stuff. Edit, EDIT!

## This is about my parents, and John Kerry

Verbal editing (or lack thereof) causes trouble for comedians and non-comedians alike. On my mom and dad's first date, they got hamburgers and were eating them in the front seat of Dad's '46 Plymouth ('cause Dad knows how to party). He was nervous and trying to make a good impression (too late), so when Mom looked for something to wipe her hands on, Dad said, "There are some sanitary napkins in the glove compartment."

Smooth, Dad. Unfortunately, there's no delete key for the mouth.

Mom replied diplomatically, "Well, I'm glad they're clean." And thus was born a relationship dynamic that would continue for more than thirty years. Dad goofs, Mom covers.

If U.S. Sen. John Kerry were a better editor he might have been president. In his ill-fated 2004 presidential campaign, in the midst of relentless accusations of "flip-flopping" on the issues, Kerry made the following off-hand, on-camera, soon-regretted comment: "I voted *for* the 87 billion dollars *before* I voted against it." Why not just get drunk on the way to your AA meeting?

In a way, it was a money-saving, career-saving comment. He saved Republicans thousands of dollars on ad writers, and saved his own career . . . in the Senate.

On the other side, I can't figure out whether President George W. Bush is a fantastic editor or a horrible one, there's evidence of both. Even the most recognized presidential acronyms -- FDR, JFK, LBJ -- require three letters. W did it in one. That's good. He also possesses the unique ability to edit most of a long sentence into a fun, new word, like "misunderestimated." On the other hand he's one of the few people who has ever needed to edit *within* a word itself, e.g. "subliminable" needs one less syllable.

## This is about other stuff

Of course, there are some things that are funny but not relevant.

Hands-free cell phones. Great for driving. Weird if you're standing at a urinal... and someone is using one . . . and you don't know that. I walked into a restroom, saw a guy standing at a urinal, looking down, saying, "Hey, how ya been? I missed you." I thought, "No way. He is NOT talking to . . . oh, it's a *cell phone*. Thank God."

See what I mean? That paragraph is potentially funny but not even remotely relevant to this chapter. If you're a comedian and you think it's funny (big if), you keep it. And like anything, if it doesn't fit your life, your values and your priorities, meaning it's not relevant, take it out.

I'm willing to bet that as you've been reading this something has come to mind about your life that you know you need to take out. So do it already! Most of us know exactly what we need to do... and just don't do it.

## Was there a point?

Friends, here is the big bottom line: Taking out anything that isn't funny or relevant is how you get from good to great, how you get to the next level in anything. I did a show in Minneapolis and a trusted friend and colleague who has booked me to many events sat down with me afterward. She knows my show well. I had just received two standing ovations and a ten-minute encore. Ready to receive my "due praise," I sipped from my glass and looked at her hopefully.

She said, "Ok, Mike. That was good. Now let me tell you how you can be great."

I thought, "Excuse me?" But as I said, greatness feeds on feedback, so I just listened as she pointed out what I had to agree were a few slow spots in my show. And this was years after first applying Kier's advice. The fact is, there will always be room for improvement.

You see, this is not a one-time thing. Whether you aspire to be a comedian, a parent, a teacher, a corporate executive, or president of the United States, taking out anything that isn't funny or relevant is a lifetime pursuit, a championship habit, a cornerstone of excellence. It's the difference between rock bands and the Rolling Stones. It's the difference between bicycle riders and Lance Armstrong.

Time is life. If something is worth your precious time, it is worth doing right, right? Take out anything that isn't funny. Or relevant.

I have only one fear, though . . . will this chapter survive the cut?

**Ask yourself...**

1. As you read this chapter, what one thing jumped into your mind as something you know you need to take out of your life? When will you get rid of it?

2. Think about your career and name five things you need to take out, edit, or just stop doing. When and how fast can you get rid of them?

3. Now think about your personal life and relationships and name five things you need to take out, edit, or just stop doing. Who is in your life who shouldn't be? Who is not in your life who should be?

4. What do you do that makes you good, but keeps you from being great? Are you willing to risk letting go of it?

5. How will you start today taking out anything that's not funny or relevant?

# About the Author

### Mike Rayburn

Mike Rayburn was born breech with six fingers on his left hand. Thus destined to be a little odd and work with his hands he has fulfilled his birthright: Mike Rayburn is the World's Funniest Guitar Virtuoso!

A regular headliner at Carnegie Hall, Mike's "Classically Trained, Comically Derailed" show is an odyssey of masterful guitar, clean, universally appealing comedy, and musical combinations God never intended.

As a captivating keynote artist Mike Rayburn uses his music-based comedy and his formidable guitar skills to challenge audiences to leap beyond their perceived limitations in the most unique, hilarious, and musically amazing keynote you'll ever experience. Mike draws from his experiences as a comedian, adventurer, business owner, author, philanthropist, husband and father.

### Contact Information:

Mike Rayburn
Quantum Talent
Phone: (843) 839-1668
www.mikerayburn.com

# Eureka! Unlock

# Your Natural

# Creativity

# With Humor

## By Bill Stainton

"Where on earth do you get your ideas?"

For fifteen years, that was the question I heard more than any other.[1] That's because for fifteen years, I was the executive producer of the No. 1-rated local comedy TV show in America, Seattle's *Almost Live!* Together, my staff and I wrote and performed nearly two thousand comedy sketches and well over ten thousand individual jokes. My friend Drew

[1] With the possible exception of "Are you always this irritating?"

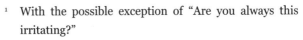

said we were "the most creative people in Seattle."[2] I'm not sure I'd go that far, but it was true that when Seattleites made their mental lists of "creative" and "non-creative" people, we were usually in the former.[3]

And that's too bad, because that distinction is a completely artificial one. The truth is that everybody is creative (except, perhaps, the guy who wrote the *Police Academy* sequels).

Some years ago, researchers surveyed two groups of people: "creatives" and "non-creatives." They wanted to see if they could isolate any trait that separated the two. They looked at factors like: did their parents read to them when they were young, do they play a musical instrument, do they prefer their peanut butter smooth or chunky (ok, I made that last one up). As it turns out, they *did* isolate one—*and only one*—trait that distinguished the creative people from the non-creative people, and it was this:

The creative people believed they were creative.

That's it!

So if that's all there is to it—if we're all naturally blessed with this "creative gene"—why did people think my staff and I were so much more creative than others? I think it's

---

[2]   Of course, my friend Drew also laughs uncontrollably whenever I say the words "tapioca pudding." Face it, my friend Drew is a moron.

[3]   To answer your question: No, to my knowledge, no Seattleite ever actually made such a mental list.

because people subconsciously realize there is a powerful link between creativity and humor. I mean, when you think about it, they're really two sides of the same coin:

- Both tend to take two or more ideas that don't seem to belong together, and combine them in a surprising way
- Both are commonly thought to be a "gift" possessed by the "few"
- Both have a letter count that's a multiple of five (and so we toss a bone to the math geeks)

The bottom line is that the mental process of creating humor (a joke, a sketch, a cartoon) and the mental process of coming up with an innovative solution to a business or personal problem (your boss, your car, your spouse) is virtually the same process! Even the same brain functions are involved: same chemical reactions, same electrical impulses, same synapses.[4]

This means you can boost your creativity with a few "tricks of the trade" from the humor biz. In fact, when I'm working with clients on creative thinking skills, we often use the very same techniques I use in my humor writing workshops.

And that's what this chapter is about: finding fun ways

---

[4]  The bone now passes to the neurology geeks.

to exercise your "creativity muscle"—that part of your brain that comes up with the innovative, ground-breaking ideas that will both entertain your dinner guests and make you rich by Tuesday—using humor as the medium!

Specifically, we're going to play with three "big concepts" of creative thinking.

## Big Concept #1: The More the Merrier, or Why 10 x 20 = 8

When I was producing *Almost Live!*, we had a regular segment called *The Late Report*, which was a fake newscast (like the *Weekend Update* segment on *Saturday Night Live*). Every week, each of ten writers wrote at least twenty jokes apiece for this segment. That's upwards of 200 jokes...out of which we chose *eight*. Eight out of 200. Now, I'm no math whiz, but that's fewer than half!

"Wow," you're thinking. "You guys must have been really crappy comedy writers!"

That's entirely beside the point.

And the point is this: The key to generating creative ideas is to generate LOTS of ideas! In other words, when it comes to creativity, quantity *leads* to quality. In the arts as well as in business, the most successful innovators tend to produce an incredible number of ideas...most of which don't make the final cut. We all know the story of how it took Thomas Edison five thousand (or ten thousand, or seventeen billion, depending on which source you read) attempts to find a suitable filament for the light bulb. I probably would have given up after three, which may partially explain why Edison has 1,093 patents and my total remains steady at zero.

But that's the problem—most of us tend to give up after we find two or three answers to the question at hand. (Ok—*most* of us give up after just *one!*)

So let's teach our brains how to start looking for not only the "second right answer," but the third, fourth, fifth, and beyond.

### Humor "Trick of the Trade" #1: Collecting Captions

Here's a great way to get your brain into the habit of generating lots of ideas. Find a single-panel cartoon (maybe an old Far Side cartoon, or nearly anything out of The New Yorker). Cover the caption before reading it. Now, look at the cartoon and come up with your own captions. And don't stop at just one or two. Set a quota for yourself, and come up with 15 or 20. A quota is very important. Edison, for example, placed a quota on himself for new ideas. He set a goal of one minor invention every ten days and a major invention every six months.[5]

---

[5]  For Edison, a major invention would be something like the phonograph, or motion pictures. A minor invention would be something like...I dunno...maybe dental floss.

Incidentally, this cartoon caption game is a wonderful way to get your entire workplace into the habit of generating lots of ideas. Post one cartoon a week, sans caption, with a blank sheet of paper below it. Encourage your team to come up with as many captions as possible. I guarantee the results will not only make you laugh, but will be a great creativity workout!

## Big Concept #2:
## Strange Bedfellows, or Why that Medieval History Minor Wasn't a Total Waste of Time

Sometimes you find the best ideas in the strangest places! Not too long ago, I was trying to move a refrigerator by myself, and it wasn't going well. (Yes, I could have asked a friend or two to help, but all my friends are imaginary—except for Drew, and we've already established that he's a moron.) A few days later, I happened to be reading a book about how a 15th century architect (Brunelleschi, if you must know) solved some weight and balance problems while building a huge cathedral dome in Florence, Italy. I saw a connection, and now my refrigerator, having been successfully moved, is sporting a magnificent new Renaissance dome.

Now, don't misunderstand me...I'm not suggesting you need a degree in Italian architecture. All I'm saying is that true creativity very often lives at the intersection of wildly divergent avenues. And the more divergent these avenues are, the more creative the idea or solution usually is.

Did you know that people who are fluent in multiple languages tend to be more at home with divergent ideas than others?[6] That's because these polyglots (and really, couldn't we have come up with a better sounding word for people whose entire raison d'etre is words?) tend to look at situations from a number of different perspectives. In fact, Leonardo da Vinci (no slouch in the creativity department himself) believed that to fully understand something, we need to view it from at least three different perspectives.

When I was hiring writers for *Almost Live!*, I always looked for people who had a wide range of interests. If I could find somebody who was versed in the Balkans, butterflies, and beets, I knew I'd found somebody with strong creative potential. It's not that we were often called upon to write comedy sketches about the Balkans (although beets, oddly enough, did come up on more than one occasion); it's just that people who have a wide range of interests tend to find creative connections that more myopic people just can't see.

[6]   No, Pig Latin doesn't count.

## Humor "Trick of the Trade" #2: Those nutty nouns

So how can we use humor to develop this "multiple perspective muscle"? How can we learn to see connections that others miss? Here's a great exercise that I use in my humor writing workshops. Take a blank sheet of paper. In one column, make a list of five nouns at random. In another column, make a list of five different nouns. Now, simply pick one noun from Column A and one from Column B, and come up with as many possible connections between the two words as you can. For example, if your two words are mango and love, your list might begin something like this:

- A person who loves mangos
- A person who expresses his or her love for another with a gift of mangos
- An exotic woman who falls in love with a man named Mango
- Two mangos falling in love with each other
- "The love of mangos is the root of all evil"
- A song with the title Mango Love
- Mangos as an aphrodisiac
- A "man" who "goes" to find love ("man" + "go" = "mango")

You get the idea. Again, this little game is even more beneficial when you give yourself a quota (and don't be a wuss—make it a big number, like 30 or more).

This is also a great workplace exercise. The next time your team has to work on a challenging problem, try playing the "Nutty Noun" game first as a "creativity warm-up." It'll really help get those innovative ideas flowing!

### Humor "Trick of the Trade" #3:
### Finding Gold in the Morning News

Here's a trick I learned when I was writing for *Almost Live*! and was looking for fun ways to combine different elements into a creative, comedic idea. In fact, I still use it when I'm writing a customized humorous keynote presentation. I pick up a copy of the morning paper and choose two articles at random, preferably from different sections.[7] Then I read both stories, jotting down as many connections as I can find. Granted, some of the connections are pretty dumb, but I write them all down anyway. You never know which "dumb" connection might be just the spark you need for that great, innovative idea. The one that will make you rich by Tuesday.

---

[7]  If you live in an extremely small community and your paper only has one section; and not only that, it only comes out once a week; and not only that, but the section it *does* have is mostly ads for trucks...well, what can I say? We play the hand we're dealt.

But now let's kick this little trick into high gear. As you're reading your articles and finding connections, try to connect them as well with some issue or problem you're currently working on. How, for example, might an article on the opening of a neighborhood spay-and-neuter clinic (hand to God, that's the article I'm looking at right now!) relate to the latest crisis in your workplace?

The moral? When you're searching for a creative solution, try looking in the most improbable places—and you just might find it!

## Big Concept #3: Shatter the Filter, or Why You Need a Bigger Toolbox

Have you ever heard the adage, "If the only tool you have is a hammer, you'll see every problem as a nail"?[8] What this means, of course, is that we tend to look at our life's situations through the filter of our life's experiences. For example, if an entomologist[9] spies a cockroach,[10] he or she is likely to see it through a certain filter. Now, if an epicure[11] spies a cockroach,[12] he or she is likely to be staring through

---

[8] Said by behavioral theorist Abraham Maslow, who also said, not as famously, "Does this thing look infected to you?"

[9] An insect specialist

[10] An insect

[11] A lover of fine food

[12] A filthy, unappetizing bug

a completely different filter. Same cockroach, different conclusion (particularly for the cockroach). The point is, the epicure is all but incapable of seeing the cockroach through the eyes of the entomologist. The epicure, in other words, is limited by his or her filter.

In order to truly unlock our creative potential, we need to shatter these limiting filters. We need to teach our already creative brains to swim in uncharted waters. How do we do that? With humor, of course!

### Humor "Trick of the Trade" #4: Flip it Around

The groundbreaking comedy show, *Monty Python's Flying Circus*, once did a sketch where everybody on the planet was Superman, except for one person who was a simple bicycle repairman. The Supermen were all awestruck by Bicycle Repairman's amazing ability to fix a broken pedal. What's the normal filter? That people are ordinary, but Superman is extraordinary. By flipping it around, the Monty Python team was able to shatter that filter. You can do the same thing—and have fun at the same time! Here's how:

Think of some common assumptions that you carry with you every day. They might include things like:

- The customer is always right.
- The more accurate the watch, the better it is.
- Exercise is good for you.
- The parole officer is my friend[13].
- Footnotes are annoying.

Now let's have some fun! Flip these around and play "What if?" Think of what things might be like *if*:

- The customer is always *wrong*.
- The less accurate the watch, the better it is.
- Exercise is *bad* for you.
- The parole officer is my *sworn enemy*[14].
- Footnotes are a welcome and *humorous diversion.*

I guarantee you'll come up with some funny situations. But more important, you'll be shattering your limiting filters. So the next time you're facing a dilemma in your life, try flipping it around and playing "What if?" You'll soon start seeing the situation in a new light—and when you do that, you open yourself up to the possibility of true creativity!

[13] If this particular one resonates with you, I encourage you to read the chapters on "humor and stress," or, even better, "humor and staying out of jail."

[14] Remember, this a game only. The parole officer really *is* your friend. Now put down the bat and take your pills.

## Remember...

...creativity is not a gift reserved for the few. It's a skill we all possess, a skill that improves with practice. And, whether you're the producer of *Almost Live*, a purveyor of produce,[15] or the president of General Electric, the best practice for creativity is humor!

## Exercise YOUR Creativity Muscle!

1. **Generate LOTS of Ideas (The More The Merrier)**
   • **Collecting Captions**
2. **Look for Unusual Connections (Strange Bedfellows)**
   • **Those Nutty Nouns**
   • **Finding Gold in the Morning News**
3. **See Things Differently (Shatter the Filter)**
   • **Flip it Around**

---

[15]   Final bone: the fruit and vegetable geeks.

# About the Author

## Bill Stainton

Bill is an expert in the use of humor to get a message across more effectively. A veteran of the back-stabbing world of television, he's won 29 Emmy awards for his work as a producer, writer, and performer. He's written for HBO, Comedy Central, NPR, and The Tonight Show, among others. Now he works with individuals and organizations that want to stretch their comedic and creative muscles for greater success.

Bill has authored nine corporate training programs which are distributed worldwide, and is also the author of the books *The 5 Best Decisions the Beatles Ever Made: A Handbook for "Top of the Charts" Success*, and *Bombproofing: How to Use Humor on the Platform Without Falling on Your Face*.

Bill's Customized Humorous Keynotes have audiences rolling in the aisles with humor written just for them. And his keynote presentation, The 5 Best Decisions the Beatles Ever Made, enlightens organizations with five key tools to achieve "top of the charts" success.

## Contact Information:

Bill Stainton
Ovation Consulting Group, Inc.
www.OvationConsulting.com
888-5BEATLE (523-2853)

# Flying Potatoes and Exploding Soda: The Secret to Creating Unforgettable Learning Experiences

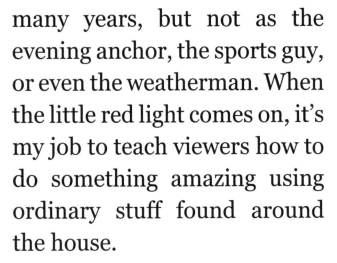

**By Steve Spangler, CSP**

I've worked in television for many years, but not as the evening anchor, the sports guy, or even the weatherman. When the little red light comes on, it's my job to teach viewers how to do something amazing using ordinary stuff found around the house.

What amazing things, you ask? Oh, like how to make a high-powered potato launcher out of pencils and straws or how to make a 2-liter bottle of soda erupt into a 12-foot fountain of fun. That's right ... you guessed it ... when the red light comes on, I become the science guy – a modern-day Mr. Wizard.

But my first job was not in television. Fresh out of college with a teaching certificate in hand, I found a job in an elementary school teaching science. It didn't take long for me to discover that my style of teaching was somewhat different from my colleagues, who spent most of their time running off worksheets in the copy room. My kids laughed a lot (almost too much at times), and this soon caught the attention of neighboring teachers and their kids, who were more than a little curious.

One colleague asked, "How can your students be learning when they're laughing so much?" Hmmm... I wonder if laughter and learning go hand in hand?

The answer is, yes!

## Electrifying Topics

I have to attribute most of my success as a teacher to my first class of third graders. Over the course of nine months, they taught me the importance of using humor to create experiences that transcended the four walls of the classroom and somehow made it to the dinner table as a topic of conversation.

"What did you do in school today?"

"Not much. Oh ... I remember something ... Mr. Spangler made us get into a big circle and hold hands ... then he shocked us with 50,000 volts to teach us about electricity."

"Are you OK?"

"Sure. He said it's normal if I forget my name and drool on my shoes whenever someone uses the microwave oven. It's just a side effect from the electricity."

I got lots of calls from parents that first year of teaching, and it didn't take long for word to spread that things were a little different in the new teacher's class.

One of those parents happened to work for the NBC affiliate in Denver. She invited me to the station one day after school and asked if I would bring along a few science experiments from my class ... including that shocking machine. In no time, I had a group of television executives making slime, shooting potatoes, and holding hands in a big circle while I delivered the shock. That one command performance opened the door for me onto a much bigger classroom. I went from 23 kids to more than a million viewers each week as the host of a nationally syndicated children's program called *News for Kids*.

My executive producer spelled out my mission in the clearest terms possible: "Your job is not to teach science. Your job is to grab the viewers' attention and show them that learning is fun. Make them laugh, and the learning will follow." These marching orders soon became my mantra and the advice that I give to parents and teachers today.

## 3-2-1 Blast Off!

As part of a promotional tour for the show, I found myself visiting children in schools across the country with my bag of cool gadgets and science demonstrations. Let's just say there's nothing terribly glamorous about doing school assemblies. The best-case scenario is that a bunch of kids are crammed into the cafeteria and forced to sit on the floor, while the guest speaker is forced to shout because the P.E. teacher is using the microphone as a doorstop.

On one particular occasion, the setting was an elementary school in the heart of Salt Lake City. Nearly 700 children squeezed their way into the cafeteria, and the principal's introduction was nothing short of inspirational.

"Hey kids ... listen up. There's a guy here who wants to show you something, and I want you to be good for a change. If I catch anyone throwing stuff at the speaker like you did last time, I'm shutting this circus down." Turning to me: "OK, they're all yours."

With an introduction like that, things could only get better. I had never taught kindergartners, but I soon learned that these little people have a tendency to grab parts of your body as a sign of affection. I did most of the show with a 5-year-old latched onto my leg. I was thankful the kids liked the demos, and I survived my first of two presentations. As the children began to file out of the room, I noticed that one kindergartner was not ready to leave. In fact, he wanted to talk to me. As he approached me, I could tell he was a little nervous. He squirmed as if it might be time to find a bathroom. As I kneeled down, he began to talk.

"Ummm ... hey guy. Guess what?"

"What?"

"I like rockets."

"Me, too!"

"And you know what else? I know how to make a rocket ... and some day I will make a rocket that can fly to the sun!"

Well, here's a tough fork in the road. I can't tell him

*no* because I would crush his dream, and I can't say *great* because I would be lying. They just don't teach you this stuff in college! I looked him in the eyes, and with compassion in my voice said, "I like your idea ... but if your rocket gets too close to the sun, it will melt."

He looked at me the way only a kindergartner could and said, "I'm doing it at night, duh!"

It was as if I had swallowed the bait and he was reeling in the catch of the day. The best part is that I had heard that joke years before, but I had never heard it told by a kindergartner!

Then the light bulb in my head went on. Behind every funny kindergartner there's a funnier person called a teacher. I immediately looked over the sea of kids to find his kindergarten teacher looking at me with a huge grin as she mouthed "Gotcha!"

I turned my attention back to the little comedian and said, "You are so funny!" His reply was tinged with apprehension: "I don't know why everyone thinks that joke is so funny."

What? Didn't the kid get it? Then it hit me like a ton of bricks. This little boy still *believed*. In his way of thinking, all things are *possible*. A joke that was so funny to me and his teacher offered little in the way of humor to him because his world was filled with limitless possibilities. What a concept!

Before leaving, his teacher and I shared a laugh, a hug, and the promise that we would never lose our child-like joy of learning.

That's So Dumb!

After almost eight years of teaching, I thought I had a pretty good handle on what makes kids tick. Then my wife blessed me with our first child. His name is Jack, and he's filled with a genuine sense of wonder.

Occasionally, I have the privilege of being the "helping dad" at Jack's preschool. I don't know how much "helping" goes on, because when I'm at school I find myself playing with the kids. It doesn't take long to forget my writing deadlines or lesson plans because I'm so caught up in the art of playing.

Oh, yes ... there is an art and science to playing. One day, I zoomed in on the building blocks, where I found a little guy who was having trouble keeping his structure from falling down.

It was helping dad to the rescue!

I made a recommendation  that we use big blocks on the bottom of the tower to make it more stable and to keep it from falling. Then we could build upon this solid foundation to create a building taller than anything the preschool had ever seen.

He stopped me in mid-sentence, looked at me with the eyes of a 4-year-old, and said, "That's so dumb! It's supposed to fall over."

What was I thinking?

What else did I learn? Toy cars can fly. Red paint is boring, but red and green paint mixed together is cool. It's more fun to color outside the lines and leave the inside white. It's fun to paint your hand. And it's really fun to misname everything! Call the fish a hamster or the bird a flying alligator and you hit a nerve.

Soon I found myself dressing a T. rex in Barbie clothes and calling it Diana Sawyer. I was learning the art of 4-year-old playtime.

As teachers and parents, we must remember that playing and learning go hand in hand. It took a simple experience like this to remind me that I didn't need to have a structured activity or worksheet to make a discovery, to explore something new, or to just to have fun. I needed this experience to remind me that I must MAKE the time to laugh and play so that I can continue to learn and grow as a parent and a teacher.

## The Science of Humor or...
## How To Make a Diet Coke Explode

Yes, this would be the perfect opportunity for the "science guy" to launch into a discussion about the science of humor — to quote amazing statistics and to expound upon the volumes of brain research revealing the incredible psychological and physiological ramifications of humor. NOT!

Let's face it, if I were that smart, I would not be blowing stuff up on morning television as a means of entertaining the masses as they drink their first cup of coffee. I guess I don't need statistics or high-level research to convince me that humor is one of the most effective tools we can use to create unforgettable learning experiences.

This is the perfect opportunity, however, to share something that you can try at home or at the office to learn more about the *science of humor* – literally! What kind of science teacher would I be if I didn't try to teach you a little chemistry?

You'll need a 2-liter bottle of Diet Coke or Pepsi and a roll of Mentos candy. You might have to do some looking to find this candy, but your efforts will pay off. This "learning experience" is best performed outside, as you'll soon see.

Gather friends, co-workers, kids, or just a bunch

of people you don't know around the bottle of soda. Remove the Mentos candy from the wrapper as you explain that you have discovered how to make a new flavor of soda. Twist off the soda cap. The goal is for you to drop all of the candy into the bottle at one time. I use a piece of scrap paper to form a tube. Fill the tube with the candy, keeping your finger on the bottom of the tube so that no candy falls out. Ask everyone to move in close to the bottle. Position the paper tube directly over the opening of the bottle, and when you're ready, drop all of the Mentos into the soda.

Oh, and one more minor detail . . . run!

There's just something humorous about watching people react as a 12-foot stream of soda erupts from the bottle. Mentos have this chalky quality that pulls the carbon dioxide gas out of the soda and causes the incredible eruption of gas. If chemistry class had been this much fun, you might have slept less and learned more.

Just give it a try, and I promise you'll never look at a roll of Mentos the same way.

# It all adds up

So, what can you learn by using humor in the classroom and out there in life? Hopefully, by now you know never to invite a guy holding a roll of Mentos and a bottle of Diet Coke to your house for dinner — but that's not all.

More important, you'll learn it's possible to tap into a kid's natural sense of humor and awaken an enthusiasm for discovery and learning.

You'll realize that a rocket ship *could* travel to the sun ... if you believe it's possible. By using the power of humor to create unforgettable learning experiences, you rekindle a childlike sense of wonder — in both children and adults —right before you turn them into a sticky mess from that stupid exploding-soda trick.

Don't worry, they'll be telling the hilarious story for years to come.

# About the Author
## Steve Spangler, CSP

Steve Spangler is known as a teacher's teacher who shares his passion for learning in the classroom, on the platform, and through the airwaves. Over the last 10 years, Steve has made over 240 network television appearances as an authority on how to make learning fun. His eye-catching science demonstrations and creative insights earned him an Emmy as the host of NBC television's News for Kids in 1997. Steve continues to use the airwaves as his classroom to reach over a million viewers each week as the "Science Guy" on KUSA-TV in Denver. Learn how to do something truly amazing by visiting his website at www.SteveSpanglerScience.com

## Contact Information:
Steve Spangler
Steve Spangler Science
Phone: (800) 223-9080
www.SteveSpanglerScience.com

# How To Get More Humor in Your Life Without Being a Clown

### By Patt Schwab, Ph.D., CSP

If you're on record bragging, "I'm at my best wearing a funny nose and polka-dot clothing," skip this chapter.

But if you're thinking, "All this stuff about adding humor to my life is dandy, but I'm not a comedian — and frankly, I don't *want* to become one!" then this chapter is for you. You don't need to be a comedian to live a laughter-filled life — you just need to employ one or more of the following easy humor hints.

## Hint #1: Create Playful People

Create an atmosphere that allows the playful, inventive, supportive side of your kids, friends, and co-workers to come forth. They'll create the humor for you. Laugh at their jokes and antics. Encourage them to share their mirth at meetings, meals, and other meaningful moments. It is as important to respond to the humor in others as it is to create humor.

If the folks around you are not already playful, encourage them with a leading line like, "Tell me something funny that happened today."

Be prepared for it to bomb the first five to ten times you use it. (If you said, "Tell me something crummy that happened," or "Tell me something that ticks you off," most folks could rant for 20 minutes. They are seldom prepared, however, to share good stuff.)

Keep asking for something fun, and eventually, wonderful things will start to happen. Co-workers will stop by your desk to share a funny anecdote from a staff meeting. Cartoons and silly cards will suddenly appear in your in-basket. A subordinate will fill you in on a personal success or relate a cute thing his toddler did that morning. When you go home, your own kids will have upbeat, positive things to tell you about.

Recently I received two unsolicited pages of solid gold in the mail – solid-gold country-western song titles, that is. Things are said in country-western music that don't get said anywhere else. (And they probably shouldn't be.) The list included such titles as "I Still Have Her Body, but I Think I've Lost Her Mind," and "Hannibal Crossed the Alps, but I Can't Get Over You."

When you create funny people in your life, this stuff comes for free! Encouraging others to share their humor is a gift from you to them.

## Hint #2: Share the Funny Stuff

When funny stuff happens, talk about it. One sophisticated human-resources vice president with a company I've consulted for assured me, "This is the corporate headquarters. Nothing funny ever happens here." Yet, a few minutes of questioning in the adjacent accounting office revealed an elaborate hoax in which a teddy bear mascot had been stolen and a series of ransom notes were left demanding that four dozen homemade cookies be delivered to the men's room at 8:16 a.m. on Monday, or "un-BEAR-able things would happen!"

The cookies were delivered, and the bathroom surreptitiously staked out. A variety of men, including the oh-so-solemn CEO, used the facility under the suspicious eyes of women trying to look like they had a reason to loiter outside the executive washroom. No one emerged with the cookies, but at the end of the day, a scout entered the bathroom and found them gone. A note on the mirror directed them to the bear -- tied up and gagged (but otherwise unhurt) -- in a bin on the loading dock.

The sad part (aside from the traumatized teddy bear) was that this episode played out over a week, and no one in the adjoining executive office knew it was happening. In fact, the accountants deliberately kept it from them for fear of being penalized. By being unreceptive to fun, the organization lost a chance for some easy team building.

(P.S. It was later discovered that the bearnapper had entered the men's room, hidden the cookies in the room's false ceiling, and safely retrieved them the next day.)

## Hint #3: Celebrate Others

Share your humor in ways that celebrate others. Sure, give awards for traditional accomplishments, but what's to stop you from awarding prizes for "Best hair," "Cutest cubicle photo," "Most resilient," or anything else that strikes your fancy?

Encourage staff to send outrageous postcards to the office from their vacations. Hold contests to see who can bring back the best "tacky tourist" gifts. (My personal favorite was a tequila lollipop with a worm inside.)

Instead of tossing out the spent pages of your joke-a-day calendar, try folding them and putting them into a "humor prescription jar" for staff or clients with an irony deficiency. Better yet, mail them anonymously to friends and co-workers. Still better, mail them anonymously to strangers in other departments. It will add a little mystery and excitement to their lives.

Slip a timely cartoon on a co-worker's desk or bring a joke book into the office instead of donuts (it will cost less and last longer). Keep a joke book by your phone for "on-hold" reading that will keep you in a cheerful mood until that tech support person finally answers (and maybe even after!).

People are busy, distracted, even conflicted, over major holidays. When you need a real break or celebration, look to obscure holidays. There is one darn near every day of the year begging to be noticed. Valuable opportunities such as Penguin Awareness Day (Jan. 20), Awkward Moments Day (March 18), Patt Schwab's Birthday Day (April 25), Eat What You Want Day (May 11), Sneak a Zucchini Night (Aug. 8), Boost Your Brain Day (Oct. 18), and even Shallow Person's Week (second week in November) should not go uncelebrated.

## Hint #4: Notice the Humor Around You

Look for the humor that is already in your life, your workplace, or your vocabulary, and draw people's attention to it. Play with a second interpretation for common expressions, e.g., "garnishing wages" might mean adding a little parsley.

Practice seeing things in a humorous context. For example, take signs literally. I particularly like the ones in laundromats that read: "Be sure to remove all your clothes before leaving."

## Other Favorites I've Seen:

- Behind the scenes in Epcot Center: "High voltage: Touch this and you're fired!"
- A misspelled notice in a shopping center near the University of Washington's dorms: "Celibate Spring"
- A sign on the door of a men's room at a sports arena: "Closed except for special events."

## Hint #5: Think Funny

Thinking funny about a problem often sparks creative solutions.

One Department of Transportation office I worked with as a consultant acknowledged what we all know — that there is a cost for cynicism and negativity. Employees bring a giant piggy bank to staff meetings, and anyone who says something negative has to "Pay the pig." It's become such fun that they even charge people who are not at the meeting but who everyone "thinks" would have made a negative comment about a discussion item, had he or she been there! At the end of the year, the money goes for a staff party. (Where, I assume, they pig out.)

Years ago, a horseback-riding accident put me in the hospital with a broken back. Toward the end of my stay, my rehab group was required to make nightly endurance treks around the floor. These were unbelievably strenuous for a group as pathetic as we were: two stroke patients, a guy with an aneurysm, another (the only one who could walk unassisted) with an IV to flush out a kidney stone, and me. Picture us shepherded by a somber nurse who periodically rushed into our line-up to keep one of us from tipping over.

One night someone (I wish I could say it was me) announced, "If we have to be in these %$^&*!! parades, let's do them right!" He then produced Groucho glasses, hats, balloons, kazoos, and assorted other accoutrements for us to use. Instantly, the dynamic changed. That night, our walk was almost 25 percent longer, other patients wanted to get in on the fun, and our somber nurse was laughing so hard we had to prop *her* up. From then on we held nightly "endurance parades," which we are convinced sped up our recovery.

## Hint #6: Collect Material

Don't be proud where you get your material. Write down jokes, personalize them, adapt them to fit the situation. Keep a joke book. No one remembers jokes; they just fake you into thinking they do. I know a guy who carries index cards with the punch lines of jokes on them. He takes a quick peek before entering a meeting or party and voila! — suddenly he is Mr. Laugh-a-Minute Party Animal.

Collect stuff and figure out later how to use it. Sooner or later, we all get stuck having to do a newsletter, a flier, or a bulletin of some sort. And when we do, we never have the right joke or cartoon. We can't remember where we saw it, it's been recycled, whatever. Avoid this problem by collecting funny items (cartoons, jokes, photos, silly awards, funny letters, etc.) as you see them.

Stuff them into an old Manila envelope or file folder and then, when your number is called and you have to produce that flier or newsletter, you'll be ready.

When we read a great book or take a stellar vacation, most of us can't stop talking about it. The same is true with collecting lots of humor — it will spill over to those around you.

## Hint #7: Create Humor From Your Life

Take events that really happened to you and make them into funny stories. Each of us has lots of personal anecdotes stored away that can bring smiles and laughter to friends, and drive points home to colleagues and clients. A bonus is that if you tell funny stories about things that really happened, you'll never have any trouble remembering the punch line!

As you develop your anecdotes, remember the two most important rules of humor:

1. Anything worth telling is worth exaggerating.
2. Never let the truth get in the way of a good story. Don't just share the good stuff: take a not-so-funny event and explore the humor in it.

For example, Gary Yohn drives a para-transit bus for the disabled in Yakima, Wash. When his wife got cancer, he shaved his head to support her. To limit the inquiries from his passengers — who, for the most part, only see the back of his head — Gary writes updates and other messages on his bald pate.

## Hint #8: Use a Rubber Chicken (subtly)

I said this chapter was for the more reserved folks, and it is. But even someone with gelotophobia — the fear of being laughed at (or, possibly, the fear of Jell-O) — can use a rubber chicken. The trick is to be subtle.

Become a "Break glass in emergency" rubber-chicken user. Keep one in the bottom drawer of your desk. Use it when you really need to change your mood, clear your brain of some frustrating person, or get a new perspective on a problem.

You don't want a lengthy heart-to-heart conversation with an office mate. You just want to solve your problem and get on with it. That's when you tell it to the chicken — chickens are great listeners. In fact, the realization that you are talking to a rubber chicken should be enough to jolt you out of your stuck place.

There may be a stressor so great that you will need to go public with your chicken, but that still doesn't mean losing your dignity. Imagine that some guy comes in, ranting and raving like Attila the Hun with a hangover. You have to be poised and professional. This is not easy to do facing a jerk you couldn't warm up to if you were cremated together. Not easy . . . unless you have your rubber chicken. You simply toe open the bottom drawer, make brief eye contact with your chicken, and relax. After all, how bad can it be? You have a chicken!

If this does not restore your equilibrium enough to handle the situation, simply place the chicken on your desk and look solemnly at it. Believe me, the guy will leave you alone. In fact, so will everyone else. (They can see you are having a fowl day.)

## Hint #9: Take Yourself Lightly

It is a myth that one must be solemn to be serious about something. We are serious about raising our children but still laugh with them. The same is true about our jobs and our responsibility to ourselves and to others. Once you get in the habit of looking at the bright side, you will find it easier to cut your problems down to a manageable size.

Learning to take yourself lightly is a powerful coping skill. I know because, as a woman who has been dumped more times than atomic waste, I've used it to come to terms with my love life. Case in point, I met my last boyfriend in Hawaii. I was on vacation, and he was the last resort.

It is important to be able to laugh at yourself. Humor can be cutting, even inadvertently, when directed at another person. A familiar corruption of something said by Abraham Lincoln goes: "You can make fools of some of the people all of the time, and all of the people some of the time — but you'll pay for it!"

Humor at the expense of others costs. It's generally safe when directed at yourself. There is, however, a caveat: Don't use jokes to denigrate yourself or your skills — use them to show your objectivity and your acceptance of yourself. For example, I frequently have to explain to people that I am 32 years old. I look so much older because I had an out-of-body experience and came back into the body of a much older woman.

Taking yourself lightly allows you to cope more gracefully with the unexpected. For example, when Jeff Jefferies was a graduate student in geriatric social work, he had a counseling assignment to get to know someone in a local senior center.

Jeff dutifully introduced himself to an elderly woman and in great detail explained that he was a grad student in geriatric counseling and asked if there was anything he could help her with.

She thought and thought while Jeff adopted his best counseling demeanor. Finally, she looked at him and said, "A few months ago I ordered these blinds from Penney's, and I don't have anyone to put them up!"

Jeff's mind did a double back flip, but luckily he landed on his feet — lightly. "Let's go," he said. "Do you have a screwdriver?"

## Hint #10: Have Fun!

The seminal hint for humorizing your life without the clown suit is to remember that it is more important to have fun than to be funny. Being entertaining isn't nearly as important as seeing the fun in everyday life. Real humor is about noticing the little things — the joys and incongruities — that are all around us. It's not a joke. It's a state of mind that reflects who you are — and who you want to become.

Become someone who gracefully connects with others through humor.

# About the Author

## Patt Schwab, Ph.D., CSP

Dr. Patt Schwab owns FUNdamentally Speaking, an international speaking company that believes in putting the "FUN" before "Da Mental!"

She shows midlevel managers and front-line staff how to use humor to increase rapport, resilience, and the bottom line. Her programs are packed with laughter, insight, and practical tips for: managing people, coping with change, and enriching work and home life.

Patt's doctorate is in Management. She is a Certified Speaking Professional—the highest earned designation awarded by the National Speakers Association. Her books include, *Leave a Mark, Not a Stain—What Smart Leaders Know About Workplace Humor; Creating Positive People in your Workplace When You Aren't the Boss; and Creating a Legacy of Laughter—60 Easy Ways to Add Humor to Your Daily Life.*

## Contact Information:

Patt Schwab, Ph.D., CSP
FUNdamentally Speaking
Seattle, WA
Phone: 206-525-1031
E-mail: Patt@FUNdamentallySpeaking.com
www.FUNdamentallySpeaking.com

# Humor is ~~not~~ a Business Word
### By Brad Montgomery, CSP

Long before I became a speaker, I was a comedian/magician. One day I was at the Post Office buying stamps. I had my paws full of press kits, and I was hoping that mailing out these envelopes would push my career to the next level. (To be honest, I was so desperate I'd have settled for pushing my career around the block.)

The postman behind the counter asked, "Flag stamps or love stamps?"

"Flag stamps," I said. "These stamps are for business."

"Oh? You can't have both at the same time?" That was one smart postman. Too bad it took me 10 years to understand how smart he was.

Get ready, folks, because here is my point in a nutshell:

Substitute "humor" for "love," and the postman was right. I'm pretty sure that "love" and "business" *can* fit together (although the tiny cubicles make it a bit of a challenge). But I am *certain* that humor and business *should* fit together.

## Your Business Is a Joke

Probably not—but it should be. Business should be fun. Most of us spend nearly as much time at our jobs as we do at home. (Unless you count the time we sleep. But if you're gonna be that nit-picky, we're gonna have some problems. Work with me here.) Because we do spend so much time working, it makes a ton of sense to figure out a way to *enjoy* our jobs, not just tolerate them. It turns out that adding humor, lightheartedness, and cheerfulness to the work day helps you get what you want. Using humor in business can improve your bottom line.

The business world has changed. Most of us will have several careers in our lifetimes, while our grandfathers had only one. Business skill sets and requirements change quicker than ever. (If you work in health care, your job has changed since you started this book. If you work in high-tech, your job has changed since you started this chapter.) Employee morale, recruitment, and retention are genuine business concerns. And the entrance of technology-driven younger generations into the workforce has changed our expectations of the workplace. (Does "business casual" mean pierced nose or pierced lip?)

If employee productivity, morale, recruitment, and retention are important to you and your business, then you already instinctively know how important it is to lighten up your workplace.

## Trust Me; This Works

Ever hear the cliché "Our business is a *relationship* business"? Well, guess what? *All* business is a relationship business. Folks choose to do business with people they like. And there isn't a person with a pulse who doesn't prefer to work with folks who know how to laugh. (Who would *you* rather work with: Yoda or Darth Vader? Jay Leno or the cop who gave you your last speeding ticket? Donald Duck or the Evil Queen from

Snow White?) You *can* laugh your way to the bank.

But the relationship between humor and business success is deeper than that. It's more than assuming that if you make a joke you'll make more sales, increase your productivity or improve your management skills. The real secret is that although people do business with people they like, they also do business with people they *trust*. And, lucky you — adding a bit of humor to your business will help folks to both like *and* trust you. (Unless your humor consists primarily of shock buzzers and whoopee cushions. Then they'll just avoid you. Unless you're only doing business with 14-year-old boys, in which case—go for it!)

Have you ever noticed that you laugh the most with people you trust? My wife and I are close friends with two other couples. We were in each other's weddings. We've had some amazing times together, both terrific and horrific. Our favorite pastime is to get together for dinner, wine, and laughter. There isn't anything we can't say to each other. There isn't any topic we need to avoid. There isn't one person among us we can't safely tease. Why? We trust each other. (Come to think of it, the wine might have something to do with it too. But I digress ...)

This connection between trust and laughter can help you in your job. We all love salespeople who can poke fun at themselves and even at their products. We love health care providers who can see the irony and absurdity in the medical world. We love teachers who can let their guards down and giggle and admit they don't know everything. The bottom line is that when we see others laugh—and when they make us laugh—we trust them more.

We like them more.

And we do more business with people we like.

### It Works? Says Who?

Tanja Pahs is a mortgage pro on the rise. One of her jobs is to approve or refuse mortgages prepared by her staff. Her staff has many incentives for getting these loans approved, so when staff members come into Tanja's office to "pitch" a loan to her, they are often uptight, nervous, and very serious.

"I just let them come in and do their thing." Tanja explains. "They sit quietly and tell me seriously why this loan should go through. When they're finished, they anxiously await my answer.

"Work should be fun, so I often let their question sit there for a moment in the silent room with us. Then I answer very solemnly, 'Well, let's see what the Magic 8 Ball has to say about this loan.'" She then reaches for that goofy toy that "predicts the future" with a small collection of answers like "Good idea," "Yes," or "Better luck next time."

For Tanja, this tiny bit of humor breaks through the tension in the workplace and replaces it with a mood more conducive to success. It's a way to give her staff permission to relax. Once the tension is broken, Tanja believes that she and the staff member can better judge what to do about the loan request. Besides, as Tanja says, "Who can be serious all day?"

Tanja is able to add humor without making fun of anybody, without a bunch of witty one liners, and without throwing a bunch of fish. (Gross!) Humor doesn't always have to be punch lines. Sometimes humor is giving yourself — and your workmates — permission to take the job less seriously.

### Wizardry on the Job

I recently spoke at a convention of people employed by the state of Colorado. The speaker who followed me was the big boss of everybody in the room. She hid in the hall with me until they introduced her, then she entered the room dressed as a wizard (pointy hat, long robe with stars and moons, magic wand). As she made her way to the platform, she threw glitter on the tables and made silly comments.

Her staff reacted with chuckles and giggles. Folks weren't falling into the aisles laughing, but they were grinning.

I thought it was a cool idea. But after talking to her later about her stunt, I thought it was an *awesome* idea. She told me that yes, it was a bit risky, but she is convinced that when her staff sees her take a fun but fairly meaningless risk, two things happen.

First, they're more likely to take risks within their jobs and to accept responsibility for themselves. In the end, they achieve more. Second, because her employees see her poke fun at herself, they are more likely to trust her with genuine concerns, including complaints. Experience has taught her she can only be a great leader if staff members are willing to share all of their concerns.

Wow. All this from a rented costume.

### D'oh, It Works for Him

Or take the superintendent of a Virginia school district

who told me he occasionally wears Homer Simpson bed-room slippers to work. He explained that when he started working in the district, there were some serious morale problems. The teachers were simply not convinced that the administration cared about them, their needs, and their concerns. The slippers help break down the walls, he believes, and are a way to connect with employees. As amazing as it seems, this man who has earned a Ph.D. uses stuffed footwear to contribute to a relationship of trust.

## Sure, It's a Bit Goofy

And how about the parole officer in Arizona who needed a way to lighten his job? This guy is not a Magic 8 Ball kinda guy ... and he certainly isn't a fuzzy slipper guy. He's more of a follow-the-rules-or-I'll-rip-your-tonsils-out kinda guy. But he is still human and needs humor to help make his job work for him.

This parole officer has a small magnet of Disney's character Goofy, and every week or two he moves it to a new location in his office, like on the air-conditioning vent near the ceiling. He also has a small dish on his desk with chocolates. When parolees come into his office, he says in a very serious tone, "Sit down. Find Goofy, and you can have a chocolate." He doesn't laugh. He doesn't explain what he means (unless they ask). And he doesn't repeat it.

What's this mean to him? For an officer with very serious and not-so-funny responsibilities, this simple game reminds him that one of his jobs is to stay sane. Humor is one of the best ways for him to keep from losing it.

## See? Laughter Saves the Day

Then there is my daughter's day care provider, Shiloh. She works out of her house, and gracefully takes care of five little kids. (And you thought the parole officer had a tough job!) A few days ago, my daughter and I were waiting for Shiloh to unlock the glass door — which of course she can see through — to let us in. As Shiloh neared the door, she shouted, "Who is it?" And then, she just broke out laughing at her own joke. (Because of course she could see us... the door was glass.)

Taking care of tiny kids can suck the life right out of you...if you can't laugh, you're done. Being playful not only enabled this woman to *survive* her job, it made it possible for her to *enjoy* her job. How cool is that?!

## Punchlines in Airlines

I'm a professional speaker, which means I travel a lot. I'm amazed at how different flight crews see humor through different filters. For example, I was recently on a small connection plane, with only about 35 seats and two flight attendants. One of the flight attendants was doing her safety announcements when she began smiling. She became really animated and fun — she was clearly enjoying herself. Eventually, we figured out that the other flight attendant, in his seat in the last row, was making funny faces at her.

I asked her about it later. She explained that she hates it when he pulls that stunt, because "It is *totally* unprofessional." Smiling and laughing? Unprofessional?

Fast-forward a week or two when I was on a small plane on a different airline. Our plane was late arriving, and for some reason our take-off was being delayed. Nerves were tight, as most folks needed this flight to be on time in order to make connections. Let's just say that folks weren't holding hands and singing in the aisles.

The flight attendant picked up the microphone and, in a Southern drawl, cut to the chase. "Folks, I know you all want to find out what's going on and how long it's gonna take. And I want to tell you. Because we're family. We're in this plane together. But here's the truth: I don't know. I've only been in Little Rock for about 25 minutes and I have no idea."

It was amazing. It was as though somebody popped the stress balloon. We laughed and relaxed. He continued:

"Folks, if you'd like, I can make something up about mechanical-this, or airports-that. I can pretend that I know stuff that I don't. Or I can be intentionally vague. But like I said, we're family, and family doesn't lie to each other. Now let's all just look out the window together and see if we can figure out what the hold-up is." More laughter.

The entire flight—which was in fact late enough to mess up most folks' connections—was punctuated by this charming attendant and his totally disarming jokes. He announced, "Now, we know you are in a hurry, so we will be flying at an altitude of 400 feet so that we can make this flight in 11 minutes." He asked us if we wanted "chicken or beef?" And gave us peanuts. He asked us if we wanted a salad. More peanuts.

When he gave me my peanut-flavored chicken, I asked him about the gold star on his lapel. He told me (OK, he told *us* ... it was a TINY plane) that he was a recent winner of the Outstanding Flight Attendant award. The entire plane erupted in applause, because it was obvious that he *was* an outstanding flight attendant. (We would have given him a standing ovation, but our belts were low and tight across our laps.)

I thought back to the first flight attendant, who thought laughter and smiles were unprofessional. The second attendant was a pro, and was recognized as such by his airline and by this planeload of passengers.

Humor not consistent with business? Oh, please. The second attendant not only enjoyed his job *way* more than his peer, but he made a difference to his customers. He earned our trust (and our continued business) through a liberal dose of humor.

## Mixing Humor With YOUR Business

Let's face it, not everyone could pull off making a planeload of upset travelers laugh. And many of us would pay huge money *not* to wear a wizard costume or Homer Simpson slippers in front of our colleagues. Maybe you're thinking, "That's fine for *them ... but what about me?*"

Well good news, Skippy, because you don't have to do anything you don't want to do. Most of us could pull off something subtle like hiding a magnet in our office. But there's plenty of stuff you can do that's even easier. And best of all, you don't have to be funny. You just have to have fun. (Check out Patt Schwab's chapter in this book for more ideas.)

# Here are four things you can do TODAY to add more humor to your business:

- Leave a funny message on your answering service. Instead of, "I'm out of the office," try: "I'm probably down the hall fighting with the copy machine" or "at the coffee machine," or maybe "playing computer solitaire and don't want to pick up, but leave a message at the beep."

- Add a joke to your e-mail signature. Or maybe add some made-up credentials to your name. Sometimes I sign myself Brad Montgomery, CSP, MTOU*. Under that, I put *CSP = Certified Speaking Professional; MTOU = Made This One Up. I'm amazed at how many people comment on my e-mail signatures.

- Consider leaving crank phone messages for both your workmates and your clients. Most adults haven't gotten a crank call for a couple of decades. Trust me, fun, spirited crank calls will make some people's business days. *"Is your re-frigerator running?"* is really funny when you're talking to somebody in a cubicle.

• This is my favorite 'cause it is so easy. Laugh. Just laugh. When you enjoy *yourself* at work, you'll give the folks you are working with the signal that you enjoy humor. Lighten up, and the world will follow.

## Don't Just Stand There

Humor works. Not only does it help us enjoy our jobs, it helps us achieve more in business. Would you want to brag on your deathbed that you never laughed at work? That work was always toil and never enjoyable? Wouldn't you rather brag that you lived your life with a smile on your face? (Or at least, in the *pursuit* of having a smile on your face.) Humor helps forge personal relationships through trust. And better relationships mean better business.

Next time you're at the Post Office, you *can* buy those cartoon stamps, or the ones with a cool rocket, or maybe even the green one with the crazy-lookin' guy with the mustache. Because, to paraphrase my favorite postman, you can have *both* business *and* humor.

# About the Author
## Brad Montgomery, CSP

Brad never planned to be a business humorist; he planned to be a lawyer. He decided to be a comic and magician for a while, then "get serious." To date—as a hilarious motivational speaker and corporate entertainer—he's still waiting to "get serious."

Brad urges audience members to "lighten up," and notice how their lives are filled with humor and magic. His programs are very funny, and leave his audiences with springs in their steps, and feeling good about themselves and their futures.

He's cracked-up folks in all 50 states and on four continents. He's published two books and authored three. And although he's proud of his many awards and national credits, he's convinced his best "tricks" are his wife and three kids.

### Contact Information:
Brad Montgomery, CSP
Brad Montgomery Productions, Inc
Denver, CO
Phone: (800) 624-4280
www.BradMontgomery.com

# Life Lessons From a Stand-Up Comedy Career
## By Jana Stanfield

It's the pre-show phone call I have with everyone who books me for a Keynote Concert. After going over goals, objectives, and sound equipment, I ask how the group heard of me.

"I saw you back in '89 in Nashville when you were doing stand-up comedy."

Visualizing this man being in the audience during my stand-up days, I'm filled with a rush of nostalgia. Nostalgia mixed with nausea. This is a piece of my past that I passed without making peace.

You often hear people say, "Look for the

lesson." For years, I've avoided looking back at my days in those dark, smokey comedy clubs, believing that part of my life would never intersect with the fine, upstanding inspirational speaker's life I lead now. I'm hoping that the passage of time will provide perspective as this phone call plummets me into an unavoidable flashback.

## Lesson 1: Hindsight is 20/20, but not right away.

Sometimes hindsight can only be achieved when you look back from a comfortable distance. Like a distance of 15 years.

As the flashback unfolds, I see myself once again inhaling the smell of cigarette smoke and stale popcorn at The Cock-Eyed Camel Club. I'm sitting at a sticky cocktail table for my first stand-up comedy class. Onstage, comedian Mike Price from LA stands in the spotlight waving his cigarette through the air for emphasis as he teaches us the secrets of timing, call-backs, and "planned spontaneity."

## He tells us:

- Don't refer to your material as jokes. A good comic makes the audience believe he comes up with this hilarious stuff "in the moment."

- Look for the funniest words you can find. Rump roast is funny. Brisket is funny because it has a 'k' in it. Words with hard 'k' sounds are funnier than words without.

- Put together the last line of your bit as a list of three. Make the last thing on the list unexpected, and make sure it's a funny word. Like this: "I took my old man fishing the other day. All we caught was a tree branch, an old boot and a brisket." Roast would be unexpected but you could never get a laugh with it because it doesn't have a 'k.' Roast. Not funny. Brisket. Funny. Omaha. Not funny. Oconomowoc. Funny.

- Once you deliver your last word, that 'k' word, that funny word, *shut up*. Don't say, "All we caught was a tree branch, an old boot, and a brisket, it was the funniest thing you ever saw. I swear we just couldn't get over it, we were laughing the rest of the day." Say brisket and *shut up*. Give the audience time to *see* what you just said. Sometimes it takes a second or two before they laugh. If they don't laugh, don't act like you were stupid enough to expect them to. Just move on.

- The longer your bit, the stronger your punch line

better be. If you bore us with a long story, it better have a killer punch line. Write down each bit and take out every unnecessary word. Then go over it again. Take out three more.

• Don't step on your punch line. If people laugh, let them laugh. Enjoy it. When you start talking again before they're finished laughing, you've just trained them not to laugh too long or they'll miss your next line. Why would you do that? If you do fewer lines and get longer laughter, that's great. You judge a comic by the number of laughs, not the number of lines.

## Lesson 2: Approach all endeavors with "beginner's mind." With beginner's mind, new information is fascinating, expectations are low, chances are worth taking, and "ignorance is bliss."

I thought comedy class would be funny. There are 15 of us in the class. No one is laughing.

Our class meets Tuesday evenings at 7:00 p.m. At 9:30, it's The Open Mic Comedy Night at the Cock-Eyed Camel. Just before the end of the first class, Mike asks, "Who's signing up to do three minutes tonight?"

For years I thought it would be fun to get up at an open mic and try to be funny. It never occurred to me that you'd write material in advance.

"I'll probably never have the nerve to do this, unless I go on tonight," I'm thinking. "Besides, no one in this class knows me, so what the heck. I'll just pretend that I'm not scared spitless."

## Lesson 3: Sometimes it's better to "go for it" without knowing how much you don't know.

Before I can chicken out, my hand shoots into the air. "I'll go up tonight."

Heads whip around to look at me. My classmates know I've never done this before. Everyone else who is signing up has experience. Class members with no experience are now making plans to stay for the show so they can live vicariously through me. Maybe they just want to see how badly a person can bomb in three minutes, which could be hilarious. I'm thinking: "As long as people laugh in my direction, I'm happy."

If I could remember anything I said that night I would tell you. All I recall is that during those three minutes of blathering in the spotlight, I get hooked. That's the only way I can explain continuing to go up week after week after class, and then week after week after the class was completed.

"I was reading in USA Today ... today ..."

The second time I go up, with a week to write material using what Mike is teaching us, I'm thinking that's a hilarious opening line. As trained, after two seconds of no reaction, I move on.

"... that Tammy Faye Bakker says she got hooked on painkillers after giving birth to her 13-year-old daughter." Pause, pause. "I'd need drugs, too, if I were giving birth to a teen-ager."

Pause, pause. Move on.

Now to the brilliant material I've ripped off from Wal-Mart greeting cards.

"I got my boyfriend a Valentine's Day card. It said, 'What would Valentine's Day be without sex?'"

Pause, pause.

"If I don't get a box of chocolate on Valentine's Day, you'll find out."

I notice that I'm experiencing more "pause, pause" than applause.

"People say that your body ought to be treated like a temple. My boyfriend likes to think of my body as an amusement park."

Week after week, Mike challenges, coaches and corrects.

"Run that Valentine's Day line again, Jana. Try it backward with chocolate as the last word. It's got a 'k' sound in it. Let us see how that hits us."

"Jana, too many words in that 'body as a temple' bit," he tells me. "Trim it."

Every week, more coaching, more correcting. Mike never tells us if our material is crap. I have to appreciate that about him. Of course our material is crap!

## Lesson 4: It's easiest to learn by example. Whether the example is good or bad, you still learn.

David Park, a geeky-looking and gifted college student comedian, is brilliant every week. "I had my colors done. There's good news and there's bad news. Good news is there are colors I look good in. Bad news is they make me look like a gay professional golfer."

Another classmate, John James, tells the audience, "I'm from Tuscumbia, Alabama, which is an old Indian word for 'nothin' funny here.' Tuscumbia, Alabama. It's like Mississippi without the glitter." He gets a few laughs but you have to wonder if they're sympathy chuckles.

Mike teaches us to start and end our routines with

something strong. "Open with something proven and easy, so that no matter how nervous you are when you go on, you know what to say and can deliver it without hyperventilating."

"Once you open with the material you're comfortable with," he tells us, "you'll calm down. That's when you try the new stuff. If all your new stuff bombs, you can save your set with your proven closer."

Mike urges us to play off whatever stereotype we fit.

Faye Woodroof, a professional comic who drops by open mic night occasionally, looks like a tastefully dressed Sunday school teacher in her 60s. With her pearl necklace, silver upswept hairdo, and her sweet Southern drawl, she says, "My husband recently asked if he was my first."

"I said to him, 'You might be. You always did look familiar."

"On our wedding night, my husband wanted to do it with the lights on," she purrs. "I said, 'Honey, stop talking and shut that car door."

They're old jokes, but I never get tired of hearing her say with her Southern lilt, "I had a physical today and I was telling my husband that the doctor says I have the legs of a 20-year-old. My husband says, 'What did he say about that 60-year-old ass of yours?' and I said, 'He didn't ask about you.'"

## Lesson 5: What works for one person might not work for everybody.

In class we try to help each other, but no one can find anything remotely humorous about my life. I'm a nice girl from New Mexico who comes from a family of farmers, teachers, and Methodist preachers. During that year at The Cock-Eyed Camel, I'm working full-time in the Nashville music business; on the side, I'm writing songs in hopes of landing a record deal. It's not that funny.

I am desperate to find a way to make people laugh at me. Remember how I said I got hooked that first night? When you get hooked like that, laughter becomes a drug you'll do just about anything to get.

You start off taking material from old joke books and telling it as though it happened to you. Soon, you're surfing comedy shows for lines you can "customize" to fit your show. Next thing you know, you see someone on TV put a rubber glove on his head and think, "I could do that."

You know you're stealing material, but you tell yourself that it's different, because he's a guy and you are a woman. You tell yourself that if you wear a sexy evening gown (emulating Faye Woodruff by playing the opposite of who you really are) and if you do "blue" material made up of words no one would expect a nice girl to say ... and then if you top it all off by whipping out that glove and putting it on your head, your set tonight will ROCK!

You try this combination a few times, and people laugh hysterically at you for the first time ever. The incredible rush convinces you that you must have more.

Soon, pulling the glove down to your eyebrows isn't enough. You open your shows with a few jokes, then within a minute you put the glove on your head and pull it all the way down over your nose. You look like a beauty queen gone bad who's on her way to rob a 7-11.

When pulling the glove down over your nose loses its thrill, you discover how easy it is to take a deep breath, shut your mouth, shoot air through your nose, and blow up the glove on your head like a balloon.

This is it!!! Week after week, the crowd goes wild. The visual of the sweet girl with the trashy humor, the sexy evening gown, and the hand balloon on her head is stunning.

With an opening like that it doesn't matter what you do next. The crowd is yours. You've established that you're willing to make a fool of yourself to make them laugh.

## Lesson 6: If you're going to climb the ladder of success, make sure your ladder is against the right wall.

Soon I'm invited to do a few guest sets at the local Zany's, the full-time comedy club. Despite the fact I've worked so hard to make it in music, I'm starting to see a future in stand-up comedy. Success is coming fast. I'm wondering if I've found my true calling.

Colleagues from the music business are coming to see the show. Soon they're bringing friends. Ironically, I'm more concerned about my sexy outfits than the hand balloon on my head. People from my church are coming, but I figure, "Hey, people from Faye's church probably come, too, and they know it's just an act for her and me. I'm doing a character, complete with costumes. It's showbiz."

Older family members visiting Nashville from my New Mexico hometown come to the show, including my dad, who cleans my car out as a surprise for me and discovers a box of neon-colored prophylactics under the seat. I explain that I bought them to try for my comedy routine, but the whole quest for laughs as this character is starting to feel uncomfortable. For the first time in a year, I'm not feeling well, so I skip open mic Tuesday. But after a week without my laughter fix, I'm back on stage in my gold strapless gown, wowing the crowd. They are AMAZED that a sweet-looking woman can get a surgical glove on her head and that she is willing to go to ANY lengths for a laugh. With lightning speed, she pulls the glove down over her eyebrows, then over her nose, and BLOWS.

If I were telling you this true story in person, I would just stop right here. For a long time. Long enough for you to guess what happened that night...

When I blew into that glove pulled tight over my nose ...So soon after a head cold.

I won't dive into the messy details.

Too draining.

It's a sticky subject.

I hate to blow your image of me.

I will only say that it was my shortest show ever in stand-up comedy. And my last.

The minister's voice on the other end of the phone line brings me back to the present, back to my desk at Keynote Concerts, Inc. I'm shocked that after what he saw, he's inviting me to do a program for his congregation. I ask how he came to choose me for the job. "I've been hearing good things about your work, and then our senior minister saw you do your Keynote Concert at a conference this past year. He came back and said you'd be perfect."

I tell the minister that I feel embarrassed knowing he was in the audience back then. As I try to explain that what I was doing then "wasn't me," we talk about grace. Methodists believe in a God of second chances.

This nice girl from New Mexico will now be flying from her home in Nashville to the place of her birth, Las Cruces, to perform a Keynote Concert called, "I'm Not Lost, I'm Exploring." A fitting title, don't you think? My songs and stories will be about how to keep joy in this journey of a lifetime, including the most important lesson I learned from my year in stand-up comedy: It's better to bomb as yourself than succeed as somebody else.

# About the Author
## Jana Stanfield, CSP

After blowing it in stand-up comedy, Jana Stanfield found a way to get paid to be herself. She now travels the globe delivering The Jana Stanfield Keynote Concert Experience: A Mental Health "TUNE-Up" To Keep You Working and Living Well. You've heard Jana's compositions on 20/20, Entertainment Tonight, Oprah, and radio stations nationwide, sung by Reba McEntire and many others. As a musician, humorist, and inspirational speaker, she performs on the world's most famous stages, from the Grand Ole Opry to Carnegie Hall. Working primarily at conferences for women and members of the helping professions, Jana has shared her Keynote Concerts in the U. S., India, Canada, the Bahamas, Australia, New Zealand, Thailand, and Singapore.

## Contact Information:
Jana Stanfield
Keynote Concerts, Inc. • Nashville, TN
Phone: (888) 530-5262
Email: Business@JanaStanfield.com
www.JanaStanfield.com

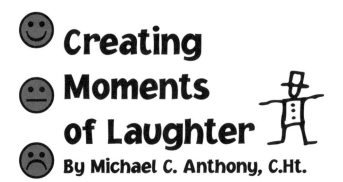

# Creating
# Moments
# of Laughter

## By Michael C. Anthony, C.Ht.

Sixteen hundred people are packed into a theater in Pennsylvania. I'm on stage opening my presentation with some "mind reading." A girl from the balcony volunteers to see if I can read her thoughts. She stands. When I ask for her name, she replies, "Cindy." I tell her she's correct.

Next, I accurately guess that Cindy has a pet turtle (can't tell you how; that's a trade secret). When I guess its name is JoJo, she screams. By now the crowd is hysterical with laughter, and I'm grinning from ear to ear. I had created a moment.

As a professional entertainer I create these moments of laughter for a living. But what I've come to understand through my study of these wonderful and instant shifts in our moods is that you don't have to be an entertainer to do it. All of us can create these moments of laughter; and all of us should.

## Planting the humor seed

I learned about the power of laughter early on. Both sides of my family have their fair share of "clowns," and I'm proud to be one of them. We like to have a good laugh any time we can. We also like to tease each other. It's all part of how we love each other.

When I was a boy, my Uncle Joe would visit from time to time. Uncle Joe was a magician, a well-known hypnotist, and one of the forefathers of balloon artistry. My brother Joe and I were always excited when our uncle was around because he would fool us until we collapsed on the floor laughing. The way Uncle Joe used his magic to create moments of laughter made a real impression on me. Even at a young age, I knew I had to find a way to generate those same wonderful feelings myself. I wanted to be able to make others laugh too. Thanks to Uncle Joe, I'd become a magician too.

When I was 19 that childhood dream got a jump start when I saw a magician on television. He blew me away; I was absolutely amazed. I had absolutely no explanation for what I saw. I slept poorly for days because I just couldn't stop thinking about those tricks. I went to the library looking for answers. (Remember when we went to the library for answers? These days, we type a request into our computer and "presto," we have an answer.)

The books I borrowed had a bunch of cheesy, easy-to-do tricks for young children – not what I was looking for. But there was something that interested me: an address for Abbott's Magic Factory in Colon, Michigan, and a mention of a catalog for magicians. "What's a magic factory?" I wondered. And, more important, "Is there really a town called Colon?"

I wrote to Abbott's Magic Factory, and for about six bucks I received a three-inch-thick catalog listing every conceivable magic trick and magic accessory. It was the magic mother lode. I spent almost everything I had on magic in those days, and you know what I received? A bunch of junk. (Well, not all the apparatus was junk, but I can't say the same about the practitioner ... )

I would practice this stuff and my friends would laugh – at me, not with me. I don't really blame them. Some of the props I bought were nothing short of ludicrous. Take the Floating Doll. (My friend Mike still laughs about that one 20 years later – talk about creating a moment.) You would cover this doll with a handkerchief, and it was supposed to float. The problem was, it only floated if the magician held onto a wire sewn into the handkerchief. It was pathetic and ridiculous. But probably the most embarrassing part was that I had spent $60 for a doll, a handkerchief, and a piece of wire.

But I practiced and practiced. One day, Mike came over and I tried out my most recent trick. He was sitting at the kitchen table when I pulled out a deck of cards. I told him to pick a card. He rolled his eyes – he'd been through this many times before. He reluctantly picked a card, looked at it, and shuffled it back into the deck.

I said, "OK, I'm going to try to find your card." I went through the deck, pulled one out and said, "Is it the six of hearts?" No. So I asked for another chance. I pulled out another card: "Here it is, the two of clubs." Mike laughed and said, "No," and then started making fun of me. He chanted "Oh

Houdini, oh Houdini" and started laughing hysterically. (Who could blame him after the Floating Doll fiasco?) I stood there apparently confused and said, "Hmmm, if it's not the six of hearts, and it's not the two of clubs, then it must be the card stuck on the ceiling." He looked up, spotted his king of spades on the ceiling, and screamed. I had created my first moment with magic. And with that one moment, I was hooked.

## Fun-colored glasses

I've been blessed to have what I consider to be the best job in the world. Sure, people like Bill Gates make billions of dollars and change the world. That's great. I may not be changing the world, but if I can change the mood of my audience and the people I encounter in my life, I've made a difference. Making somebody smile might not change the world, but I can change the moment. And if you string together enough moments...

By now, you may be thinking, "That sounds fun, but I don't do any magic tricks. I'm not an entertainer." Stop right there. All I'm talking about is creating moments of laughter – and you don't need to be an entertainer to do that.

In essence, it's about looking at life in a different way. I believe people take life way too seriously. They spend hours worrying about things that never happen. People are stressed and need more moments of laughter in their lives to get juiced. They need to start looking at life through fun-colored glasses and find the humor in everyday things, like how it always rains when you plan a picnic, or how everyone faces the doors after getting on an elevator.

Think of some of your most amazing memories. Think of good times you've had with family, friends, or co-workers. If you are like most people, most of these moments are based around laughter. We all love to laugh. Some researchers say that the average person laughs up to 17 times a day.

I've also heard that laughing 100 times is equal to 15 minutes on an exercise bike. I'm all for keeping fit, but hey, if I can spend more time laughing and less on the exercise bike, "Show me the funny!" Here's another bonus: Scientists at Loma Linda University in California discovered laughing lowers our blood pressure and fires up our immune system. (To learn more about the therapeutic effects of humor, look for Patty Wooten's chapter in this book.)

## Finding the funny

How do we fill our lives with moments of laughter? It's simple. We create them. The world is our canvas. Go out there and make someone laugh. Do it at work or at home. Joke with your spouse, your kids, even your dog. Believe me, life is much easier when you have a sense of humor. And if you can learn to laugh at little things that may not seem funny – like when someone cuts you off on the freeway, or when your restaurant order shows up incorrect – you'll find your life to be — at least a little bit — less stressful.

Life has a way of creating the demanding moments. It's our job to create the funny ones. As psychologist and philosopher William James said, "We don't laugh because we're happy, we're happy because we laugh."

So, think of something funny and create some memories for yourself and your loved ones. Here's one of mine:

My wife, Kim, and I were moving out of our first apartment. One day I had been running errands for our business while she was home packing. As

I was riding up the elevator to our apartment, I mused, "What can I do to my wife that would be really funny right now?" The idea came in a flash, as if it were a gift from above. When I arrived at our door, I looked around to make sure nobody was lurking in the hallway. Then, as quickly as I could, I dropped every stitch of clothing except my sneakers. I picked up my briefcase, opened the door, and walked in as if everything was normal. When my wife saw me come in the door she shrieked and dropped to the floor. She thought that I rode up the elevator and walked down the hallway naked. She thought I'd had a nervous breakdown.

After she regained control, we had a great laugh. Kim told me she just asked her sister to come over to help pack, but she wasn't available. The joke was almost on me. In creating a funny moment for myself, I almost created a funny moment for more people than I had intended.

Here's another fond memory:

My brother Joe celebrated his 40th birthday awhile back in Canada. I couldn't be there because I was on tour. Right before I was to go on stage for a presentation in New Jersey, I called him to wish him a happy birthday. While we were chatting, I got an idea, I got an idea, so I stayed on the phone while they introduced me.

The guy who introduced me said, "Let's have a big round of applause for Michael C. Anthony." I walked out with the phone at my ear. I'm sure the audience thought I was on an extremely important call. My brother heard the noise and asked about it. I put the phone on speaker and said, "Hey everyone, I have my brother Joe on the phone and it's his 40th birthday today. At the count of three, everybody say, 'Happy Birthday Joe.' " The crowd bellowed, "Happy Birthday Joe," and my brother was hysterical, telling everyone around him what was happening. It's not often that 500 people wish you a happy birthday. We had created another moment.

Your memorable moments don't always have to be funny. Sometimes they can be heartwarming. But I think people best remember the ones that make them laugh. I'll bet women remember the laughter they get from their husbands more than the flowers. Note to men: Stay smart. Give flowers anyway.

Laughter in, laughter out
Is life serious? Absolutely – that's why you need to have fun from beginning to end.

So pick up the phone and make a prank phone

call to a friend. Paint someone's toenails red while they sleep (sorry, Dad). Put a piece of cardboard in somebody's sandwich (got me again, Mom). Buy a can of Silly String and empty it out on a colleague. Put a big glob of peanut butter on the roof of your dog's mouth.

Fill your memory banks with laughter. Don't wait for moments to happen – create some of your own. Have you been blessed? Next time you go to a restaurant, leave a $20 bill on the table for the waitress. For a laugh, attach a string to it and yank it away as she reaches for it. Then give it to her anyway.

Go ahead: make somebody's day. Give somebody else something to talk about. You'll do both of you some good. I've always believed you get out of life what you put in. I live my life by the principle that you reap what you sow.

If you don't have anything to laugh about, go find something. The world is full of funny things and funny people. If you enjoy life most of your memories are happy ones. If you're cranky, you're spending too much time thinking about the lousy stuff. It's easy to take everything too seriously, to get so bogged down by the details that you forget that life is a fantastic, joyous ride, and we only get one shot at it. It's time to banish that negative attitude forever. Take time to smell the roses. Make a crucial investment in your life: create moments of laughter. Start from there, and the rest of the good humor will follow.

Writer and lecturer Anne Wilson Schaef said, "Laughter is like the human body wagging its tail." So I say, get out there and shake it!

# About the Author

## Michael C. Anthony, C.Ht.

Michael C. Anthony is an award-winning speaker and entertainer who believes we can laugh (really hard!) while learning valuable life-changing principles.

Using the arts of mentalism and hypnosis, Michael's mind-blowing programs captivate, inspire, and keep people talking for weeks.

In his hilarious keynote presentation, Use Your Brain...for a CHANGE, Michael trains audiences to utilize their own mental resources and create permanent change in their lives.

Michael has been seen on NBC, CBS, ABC and Fox. VH1 says "He's absolutely hilarious...the best on the planet."

**Past clients include**
Hewlett Packard,
Minolta, Home Depot
& Sara Lee

**Contact Information:**
Michael C. Anthony, C.Ht
Quantum Talent
Phone: (843) 839-1668
www.michaelcanthony.com

# Good Health IS a Laughing Matter

**by Patty Wooten, RN, BSN**

Everyone wants good health and a sense of "well being." To achieve good health we struggle to restrict our diet, exercise regularly, and try to control our stress. Wouldn't it be terrific to find a fun way to improve our health? Good news! Research shows that a sense of humor and an ability to laugh freely can help build resistance to disease. In the last 20 years, interest in the therapeutic benefits of humor has grown tremendously.

## Ancient Wisdom to Modern Science

For thousands of years societies have recognized the healing powers of humor and laughter. Because it was believed that laughter and tears gave the body a cathartic emotional cleansing, the Greeks created healing temples at Delphi, where ill people would attend the theatrical performances of both tragedy and comedy.

The Old Testament tells us that "a merry heart does good like a medicine." Now we have scientific evidence to support this ancient wisdom. Opportunities for laughter are created by hospitals and nursing homes worldwide through therapeutic humor programs that range from funny videos in a patient's room to bedside performances by specially trained hospital clowns. Other hospitals have created "comedy carts" delivered to the patient's room by a "mirthologist," who helps the patient select humor based on what he or she finds funny. The Association for Applied and Therapeutic Humor (AATH) helps people understand the latest research and learn about effective applications for therapeutic humor. The National Institutes of Health's National Center for Complementary and Alternative Medicine http://nccam.nih.gov recognizes "therapeutic humor" as a mind-body discipline that may be  effective as a complementary treatment for disease. We've come a long way since Delphi, and most of this progress has occurred  in the last 30 years.

The therapeutic humor movement began in the early 1970s after the publication of Norman Cousins' book Anatomy of an Illness, in which he shares his personal story of how laughter facilitated his recovery from ankylosing spondylitis (an autoimmune disease). At the time of his diagnosis, Cousins suspected that his high-stress lifestyle as the editor of Saturday Review may have created the internal conditions for his disease to thrive.

Cousins theorized that an emotional balance was essential to good health, and when that balance was tipped, and remained out of balance, the body experienced a disease. Cousins described an emotional continuum with catatoxic emotions at one end and syntonic emotions at the other end. "Catatoxic emotions" include fear, anger, panic, despair, and dread — common feelings during and after stress. He proposed that a life filled with these emotions could create an internal environment within the body that leaves a person vulnerable to disease. And sure enough, scientific research has proven that these catatoxic emotions contribute to hypertension, coronary artery disease, depression, alcoholism, drug dependency, and much more.

We have less research at the other end of his range. "Syntonic emotions" include love, hope, joy, forgiveness, and confidence. Cousins believed that laughter served as his "gateway" into the experience of all syntonic emotions and that this positive emotional experience created an internal environment that could enhance his ability to recover from disease. He laughed a lot, and it seemed to work. His disease entered remission and never bothered him again.

Soon after his recovery, Cousins became an adjunct professor at the UCLA School of Medicine and started the Humor Research Task Force. He raised awareness and money to support humor research, his book raised hopes, and the humor movement was off and running.

I joined the humor movement in 1974, although at the time, I didn't know it existed. My marriage had ended in divorce, and I was suddenly a single mom of a small baby. I was very sad. At the time, I worked as a nurse for intensive-care brain-surgery patients, a job that was both demanding and depressing. And just when I thought things couldn't get worse, in the first year after my divorce I was raped, burglarized, and mugged. Life was tough and, with the exception of the loving feelings I had for my son, I didn't feel much joy or hope. That's when the miracle occurred.

I was driving to work one day, trying to strengthen my spirit for the challenges I would face. I turned on the radio, and in that precise moment the announcer said, "Would you like to laugh?" That got my attention. He continued: "Would you like to help others to laugh? Come to San Diego State University and register for clown school." I quickly realized this just might be the "shock therapy" I needed to lift myself out of the joyless pit of depression into which I'd fallen. Sure enough, it worked.

For 14 weeks, I learned the art of clowning from a Ringling Bros. Clown School graduate. Painting my face helped me hide my depressed self, and I began to "act as if" life was fun and funny. My new-found clown skills gave me the opportunity to be playful and spontaneous and to enjoy life with childlike delight. I discovered that all the syntonic emotions were "just a laugh away," as Cousins had promised. I became a therapeutic humor convert through the experience of my own self-healing through laughter.

I graduated from clown school ("magna cum really

loud") and wanted to use my new skills to help others experience the emotional healing that laughter had given me. I got permission to "clown around" in a local nursing home. The residents were delighted and the nurses were surprised — surprised to see so much joy and exuberance. The nurses asked me to teach them how to help their patients laugh more.

At that point in my nursing career, I'd saved lives in the ICU and helped people die with dignity in their homes, but this new request seemed like a big challenge. So I called Norman Cousins at UCLA and described my dilemma. He introduced me to Bill Fry, Vera Robinson, and Lee Berk — the pioneer researchers whose work gave therapeutic humor strong credibility.

For the last 25 years, it has been my quest to understand how humor and laughter can be therapeutic to the body, mind, and spirit, and to help people create more opportunities for laughter in their life.

Let me tell you about what I've learned along the way.

## Power of the Human Spirit

Nurses often care for people who are able to maintain a strong spirit when they face the challenges of illness. These patients use humor to change their internal experience when they can't change the external reality of the moment. Humor can be defined in many ways, but my personal favorite is: "Humor is the ability to find joy in the face of adversity." Our sense of humor gives us a "perceptual edge" to help us find joy and happiness — anytime, anywhere.

For example, Karen came to our oncology clinic every week for her chemotherapy. After a month she had lost all of her hair and began wearing a wig. One hot summer day, however, she came to clinic without her wig, her shiny, bald head visible to all. Her T-shirt sported a variation of a Calvin Klein commercial: "I'm too sexy for my hair. That's why it isn't there." Instead of complaining about her condition, she chose to laugh about it.

Another patient I cared for in San Francisco had a scar that went from her upper chest to lower abdomen. She told me one day: "I call this Market Street because it goes from Twin Peaks (her breasts) all the way to the waterfront (her pubic area)." She could have bemoaned her disfigurement, but instead she chose humor to change her perspective and to laugh about it.

Finding humor in adversity can also be seen with people surviving natural disasters. After an earthquake in LA, a sign in front of a collapsed house advertised: "House for sale — Some assembly required." After floods along the Mississippi River, a restaurant was filled with three feet of water. A sign on the front window read: "Waitress wanted -- must be able to swim." And after a tornado in Texas blew the roof off their house, a family that had to live across town with relatives put a sign on the front door announcing: "Gone with the wind."

These stories show how a sense of humor helps us remain emotionally resilient during challenging times. This humor-powered "bounce-back-ability" from emotional distress is also replicated in our body's immune response to humor. Scientific evidence is growing to prove that joy and happiness can actually strengthen the body's resistance to disease.

Our immune system is composed of more than 30 trillion cells that move about the body looking for bacteria, virus, and cancer cells, which they then attack and try to kill. These cells have different names and different functions, but research shows that many of these cells are more effective in the presence of syntonic emotions and are actually weaker in the presence of catatoxic emotions. Research in the field of psychoneuroimmunology shows that different chemicals (called immunomodulators) are released during various emotional experiences. These chemicals "plug into" receptors on the surface of the immune cell and can then change the molecular machinery inside the cell, either enhancing or reducing the cell's strength and ability to protect us.

# Research Measures Emotional Impact

Psychologist Sheldon Cohen at Carnegie Mellon University in Pennsylvania found that happy people are three times less likely to get a cold. A study of more than 300 healthy volunteers rated their emotional state on a continuum of "happy, pleased, and relaxed" versus "anxious, hostile, or depressed."

Next, the researchers exposed the subjects to the rhinovirus that causes colds. Interviews over the next five days clearly showed that people with a positive emotional state were more resistant to getting a cold. These results correlate with the research findings of Michael Irwin at the VA Medical Center in San Diego, of Rod Martin at University of Western Ontario, and of Lee Berk and Stanley Tan at Loma Linda University in California.

Natural killer cells move about the body trying to eliminate virus and cancer cells. When these cells are active, the body is better protected. Michael Irwin's research shows a decreased natural killer-cell activity during a depressive reaction to life changes. Rod Martin found that people with negative mood states experience lower levels of salivary IgA, an antibody that protects us from respiratory infection. Research by Lee Berk and

Stanley Tan showed that mirthful laughter reduced the level of stress hormones (which have been proven to weaken the immune system), increased the number and activity of natural killer cells, and increased the concentration of salivary IgA.

Perhaps Hippocrates, the father of medicine, was correct when he said, "I would rather know the person who has the disease than know the disease the person has." For thousands of years we've known that our attitudes, beliefs, and emotions can influence our health. Norman Cousins' suspicions seem to be correct. As he told us more than 30 years ago: "Laughter serves as a blocking agent. Like a bulletproof vest, it may help protect you against the ravages of negative emotion that can assault you in disease."

## A Merry Heart

Laughter may also protect the heart. Michael Miller, M.D., director of Preventative Cardiology at the University of Maryland, presented his research at the November 2000 American Heart Association meeting in New Orleans. His study of more than 300 people (half without coronary disease and half with a diagnosis of heart attack or coronary artery bypass surgery) found that people with heart disease were 45 percent less likely to respond with laughter in awkward social situations than their healthy counterparts. They also found that those who laughed the most had a lower test score for hostility and anger. We have known for many years that anger and hostility contribute to coronary artery disease. So perhaps that ancient wisdom was correct — a merry heart IS like a medicine. Or to put it another way, a hearty laugh shows a healthy heart.

## Where's CNN?

You might be asking, "Why haven't I read about this research on the front page of the newspaper?" One reason is that the research sample sizes are too small for the results to be "statistically significant," according to the rigorous standards set by the scientific community. Financial support and research grants for studies of laughter have been small, and the cost of immune system tests is expensive, so the number of subjects studied has been limited. Even though these research studies were carefully designed and well controlled, and have been published in professional journals that require rigorous scientific scrutiny before publication, the statistical analysis for the studies are too weak to "prove" that mirthful laughter can reliably stimulate the immune system for everybody in any situation.

Stay tuned, though; we will hear more from the scientists! And, of course, don't forget what Albert Einstein told us: "Not everything that counts can be measured."

## Therapeutic Humor Movement: Alive and Well

Since graduation from clown school I have been "riding the wave" of the humor movement as it grows in both size and credibility. Eventually I made a video with Norman Cousins, clowned with Patch Adams, and completed my own research on humor and nurse burnout, which I presented at the International Society for Humor Studies in 1990. In 1985, I was one of a small group of nurses that founded the Association for Applied and Therapeutic Humor www.aath.org), which has grown to be the best resource for learning about how humor and laughter can be beneficial for the body, mind, and spirit.

The goal of my life's work has been not only to understand the scientific WHY of how humor can improve health, but also to find out HOW to apply humor therapy in the real world with real patients. Learning to laugh can lead to a happier and healthier world.

As you read the other chapters of this book, I hope your enthusiasm and understanding of humor grows so that you feel compelled to include it in your life every day. Remember, good health is a laughing matter.

# About the Author

### Patty Wooten

Patty Wooten understands therapeutic humor from the perspective of a nurse, a clown and her own self healing experience.

Her study of humor and laughter began in clown school and has taken her to five continents in the last 25 years. She has written 3 books: *Heart, Humor and Healing, Compassionate Laughter* and *Hospital Clown* to appreciate the humor and health connection.

Ms. Wooten is an informative and hilarious professional speaker who shares an important message about the healing power of humor. Healthcare professionals, patients and families alike have laughed and learned.

Patty is a founding member and past president of the Association for Applied and Therapeutic Humor and received the Lifetime Achievement Award for her contributions to the discipline of therapeutic humor.

Visit Patty's website (www.jesthealth.com), where you can find reading lists that include the published research studies mentioned in her chapter, links to other therapeutic humor Web sites, and articles Patty has written.

### Contact Information:

Patty Wooten, RN, BSN
Phone: (888) 550-5378
Email pwooten@JestHealth.com
www.JestHealth.com

# Purple Hair, Or How to Laugh About the Tough Stuff

**By Anne Barab**

You've got to laugh at the tough stuff. The sooner you can laugh, the faster you'll heal. Finding the funny in bad stuff has been a hard lesson for me to learn. I spent the better part of several decades being in a snit because some people, unlike me, were less than perfect. Bosses, colleagues, family members, gynecologists, postal workers, grocery store checkers, and freeway drivers all seemed to have enough free time to collaborate on making my life miserable. It was as if they sent out letters and made telephone calls (yes, children, there was a time shortly after the Earth cooled that e-mail did not exist) saying, "OK, you say something ugly at work, then you cut her off on the entrance ramp on Highway 75, and then five of you crowd in front of her with 27 items each in the 15-item express lane."

Clearly, I was wound a trifle too tight. God finally got exasperated and decided to teach me a thing or two about patience and good humor. The way He did this was — He gave me children.

## Be Careful What You Wish For, You Might Get Large Quantities of It

My husband and I had been married 10 years when we decided it was time to reproduce. (He's an engineer, and engineers employ a particularly effective birth control device – namely, their personality.) We carefully planned for the blessed event to occur in July 1980, during what turned out to be the hottest summer in Dallas history. With my ankles resembling cantaloupes, I vowed never, EVER to have another baby in July. And so it came to pass two years later that we had TWINS in August. God laughed.

Now, we didn't know there were two babies in there until a just few weeks before they were born. There were signs, but I just ignored them because I knew (being the perfect person I was) that something as aberrant as a multiple birth could not possibly happen to me. The Census Bureau says that Americans average 2.3 children per mom, and being the essentially lazy person that I am, I planned for someone else to raise my .3 kid.

When you're pregnant, people ask you one of two questions. The first one is "When are you due?" (meaning, "I see by your size that your suffering is just beginning.") Then when you sort of resemble a Volkswagen the question changes to, "How much longer?" (meaning, "I'm just glad I'm not you!")

I was only four months along and already sleeping sitting up, when a friend in the company cafeteria jumped right to "How much longer?" I casually answered "five months," and she spewed Pepsi through her nose. A month later, my Beloved Husband looked at me and remarked, "You don't need one of those T-shirts that says 'Under Construction.' You need one that says 'Goodyear.'" I thought that was a hoot so hand-in-hand, we marched into a maternity store, purchased a navy-blue shirt size XXXL, and had GOOD-YEAR emblazoned over the apex of my bulbousness.

Five days before delivery, as I waddled out of the bank wearing Goodyear, it being the only garment I could still fit into, an approaching man slapped his knee and chortled, "I just love a fat lady with a sense of humor!"

At that moment, I realized I had finally learned to laugh about the tough stuff. Here I was, sweating bullets in the 113-degree Texas heat, and we both just let off a rip-roaring guffaw. I nearly had an accident right then and there because I hadn't been to the bathroom in at least 15 minutes.

A week later, we had a regular day-care center going at our house with two infants and a toddler, all in diapers. Somebody was always crying, and frequently it was me. The 2-year-old flatly refused to potty-train because he claimed he only enjoyed Quality Time up on the changing table.

## Laughing about the Tough Stuff is a Skill That Can Be Learned

It was during this time of frenzy punctuated by absolute oceans of exhaustion that I developed three life principles for how to laugh about the tough stuff. Turns out, finding the humor in ordinary situations is a mindset – a skill – and can be learned. This skill makes you generally more resilient at work, at home, and at play. Here's an overview of my tips:

First, **assess the seriousness of the situation** – for example, is the blood gushing or just oozing? – and then figure out how flexibly you need to respond.

Second, **determine the global implications** – like, could your children (or boss, colleague, spouse, or innocent bystander) be arrested for what they just did to you, or will you most assuredly go to jail if you give them what you think they so richly deserve? And what exactly are the desirable implications of jail time? Is it quieter there? Does anybody need their diaper changed? Do they have nap time?

Third, **try real hard not to take it personally**. Most likely the person causing you misery is blissfully unaware that he has lobbed a grenade of anger-producing grief in your direction. Whether it explodes is entirely up to you, because you can choose to pull the pin or not (preferably not, especially if you claim to be a grown-up, because you're *supposed* to rise above the petty stuff). Now I enjoy pouting just as much as the next person, but after having kids I had to pass that luxury down to the shorter people in our household.

## So How Do You Cultivate this Skill of Finding the Funny in Tough Stuff?

OK, so now let's look at each point in more depth.

## 1. Assess the seriousness and be flexible.

Lots of time we get caught up in the moment and want mightily to resist whatever is happening that displeases us. Let's say, for example, you're driving to Big Chuck's House of Chicken for legs and a side of fat when your (colleague, friend, spouse) announces he'd rather take his cholesterol in the form of a big, juicy slab of ribs. For some people, this is an apparently life-threatening change of plans. Their mouth is all slobbered up expecting a certain taste treat, and they just can't adjust to the new suggestion.

Typically, people who are forced to live/work with this sort of inflexible person learn early on not to suggest changes of this magnitude. These are the same rigid people who don't like the new way of doing things at work, are constantly reminiscing about the good old days, and just generally complain about any tiny deviation from whatever they're expecting to happen. We'd like to avoid them, but they're everywhere. Is it possible you're one of them?

So here's my tip. Step back. Give the situation some distance. Ask yourself, "If it's not my way, will the sky actually fall? Could it possibly work? Am I being just a smidge inflexible here?" I find these are all good questions, and they help me lighten up and go with the flow when I'm feeling kind of ornery.

Back when I thought I was the center of the universe and in charge of everything, I was always ticked off about somebody not doing it MY way. I'm here to tell you that being Queen of the World is hard, exhausting work, and I am personally glad to have traded in my tiara for a more humble heart. I owe it all to being flexible whenever possible.

## 2. Look at the global implications and don't catastrophize.

Catastrophize is not an official word in the dictionary, but for me it is a verb that basically means to go off the deep end worrying about stuff that might – but probably won't – happen. Here's an example:

When the darling kids in our personal entourage morphed into brain-damaged teenagers, the section of their brain (I think it's the medulla or maybe the whiny-bellum) that controls the ability to put stuff away ceased to function. For 12 years they were required to put away their toys and clothes and junk every night. Then one morning they awoke and that ability had mysteriously vanished from their repertoire of accessible skill sets. I think all available brain cells (notice I'm polite and use the plural here) dedicated themselves to more important tasks, like talking on the phone and sleeping.

Their rooms were soon covered in a foot-high thatch of clothes, shoes, books, papers, mementos, and possibly the long-missing, presumed dead, turtle. The only reason the thatch was not TWO feet high was because they didn't own any more goods to discard on the floor. Unfortunately there was no way for me to get from our bedroom to the rest of the house without passing by their rooms, and every time I did it made me madder than a wet hen, however mad that is. You get my drift. Here's what I would think:

*Look at that mess ... how do they ever find anything clean to wear? ... they probably don't ... they just put on some stinky and wrinkled old thing ... that means they probably look awful and smell bad at school ... if they smell bad their teachers probably won't like them and, worse, will think I'm an awful mother ... if the teachers don't like them and they're smelly they won't learn enough to get out of junior high ... that means they probably won't graduate from high school either ... so of course they won't be able to go to college ... and that means they'll never get a job above minimum wage ... and we all know how hard it is to live on mini-mum wage ... so they'll probably end up in a trailer park struggling to make ends meet ... robbing 7-Elev-ens for chips and Huggies ... then finally they'll live under a bridge and maybe commit an ax murder.*

Catastrophizing is fun but not smart. Over time, I could leap directly from seeing the mess ... to ax mur-der in three seconds flat. Then, feeling totally justified, I would bawl them out right there in the hallway on the way to breakfast.

Now Dr. Phil will tell you that anger is a mask for fear, and you can clearly see that I was scared to death for these poor, brain-damaged individuals and also for myself, because I figured maybe they'd want to come back to our house to live in their predestined homeless state. As with many of the things we catastrophize about, none of this stuff has come to pass. In fact, not one of them today even owns an ax.

Life is chock full of bears and gnats. The bears will get your attention, but the gnats will drive you nuts. Most of what we obsess about is just gnats, and that's what I'm talking about here.

Tip number two, then, is to quit letting your fear of the unknown get the best of you. Even though getting yourself whipped into a frenzy of fear and anger is fun, and even therapeutic at times, and certainly a must when you're at lunch with your girlfriends, you really need to pull yourself off the edge, figure out if this is a gnat, and throw your head back laughing, just to prove to yourself that you're not a complete ninny and that you are skilled at adapting to any situation.

## 3. Don't take it personally; it's probably not about you.

For those of you who think other folks are lying awake nights planning to cut you off in traffic or park the space you were aiming for – you are giving us way too much credit. Like we even care about you! We're exceedingly balled up in our own world and can't waste valuable time making your life miserable on purpose. If we do it by accident, that's just a bonus!

As it happens, I served as an elected official for nine years. Because I was elected to office three times, I guess that makes me a politician. As some of you probably know, the word "politics" is derived from the Greek "poly" meaning "many" and "tics" meaning "blood-sucking." So I have direct personal experience dealing with "The Public."

It was my experience that "The Public" harbors a core belief that all politicians are: A. Idiots; 2. Liars; D. Thieves; or V. All of the above. "The Public" generally begins angry conversations by putting their face close to yours and calling you a name indicating your mommy and daddy were never married. This goes on for about 30 minutes.

Then when they think they've got you feeling all warm and fuzzy about them, they ask you for a favor. It's hard not to take this kind of treatment personally. I learned a lot about patience, self-restraint and listening hard for the core concern. But mainly I learned it wasn't about *me*.

## Everything Isn't About You

The disdain of "The Public," however, is nothing compared to that bestowed upon you daily by people to whom you gave birth. In the beginning, babies start out so precious, adorable, and sweet-smelling that you're perfectly willing, in fact eager, to sop up all the substances that are constantly leaking out of their many orifices. When you're pregnant the first time you are positive you are going to be an absolutely perfect parent and not make all those neurotic mistakes your parents made. And your child – ah yes, your child is going to be perfect, too. So how's that working out for you?

For us, things were going pretty well until our first child turned six – months. He happily lay on the changing table as I removed his dirty diaper. I leaned over to put it in the diaper pail, and when I straightened up, he was gone! He'd flipped right off the table and landed on his head. Oh my gosh, brain damage! I picked him up and inspected him for dents. He was strangely silent, so we raced to the emergency room, because of course this was Saturday night. Bad stuff like this never happens during office hours.

We sat in the waiting room, terrified, while the doctors worked on him. Finally, we  heard a little cry ... then another one a little stronger. At last the doctor walked out, looked us up and down and drawled, "This your first?"  Mutely we nodded. "Well, they bounce. There's no brain damage."

OK, maybe not then ...

Let's remember that the Lord commanded Abraham to sacrifice Isaac when Isaac was just 12, because if he'd waited until Isaac turned 13, it might not have been a real genuine sacrifice.

When our son hit 13, that brain damage just kicked right in.

First, he dyed his hair blue. He made one little mistake, though: He washed the dye out in the shower and turned the tub, walls, curtain, towels everything blue. I made him scrub everything until it was white again. Thereafter, he did all his important grooming in a porcelain-free environment – out in the front yard ... with the garden hose ... on a busy street corner ... maximizing the embarrassment for the parental units.

So he dyed it blue. Then he dyed it green. Then he parted it down the middle and dyed one side blue and the other side maroon. Then he bleached it – three times. Turned it white. Then he discovered that when you put purple dye over the bleach it turns hair NEON. Then he shaved his head. (Which reminds me, have you ever noticed that a bald black guy is kind of sexy-looking? A bald white guy, just looks like a big thumb.)

Then he grew it out into long, thick red curls. Red is his natural color. This hair was a real chick magnet. Just one problem ... he looked like Annie. He complained, "Mom, the greeters at Wal-Mart keep calling me ma'am. Can't they see my goatee?" Squinting, I spotted a tiny fringe. "I don't know, son. I see a lot of unwanted female facial hair at Wal-Mart."

Next he joined the high school marching band. I had no idea it was so hard to pace evenly and push a trombone slide in and out at the same time. He came home from summer practice hot, sweaty, and furious. "This is cruel and inhuman punishment, and I want to quit!" he stormed. In my best parenting voice I said, "No, son, you must complete the year so you can learn to finish what you start." Then I stepped back and waited for him to say, "Oh, thank you, Mommy Dearest, for teaching me this valuable life lesson."

He thanked me, all right. He reported me to the Child Abuse Hotline. It's real hard not to take *that* personally.

Here's the point: If I had taken all this stuff personally, my brain would have turned to mush and there might have been one or two justifiable homicides. But it wasn't about *me* at all – it was about *him*; my job was to help him find the real person he aspires to be. As a matter of fact, he's STILL wandering around out in the weeds on different continents looking for himself. (He majored in philosophy. He doesn't know why.)

## Lighten Up and Find the Funny

Most people I've run into who are annoying as the dickens and demand the most patience and good humor from everyone else around them – well, they're totally unaware that they're acting like slugs. I know – I was one of 'em for quite a while, and I am so grateful that those around me were willing to be patient and loving until I could finally drag myself out of the weeds of self-indulgent whining and inflexibility and catastrophizing and taking it personally to become at least a moderately mature adult.

So I'll leave you with this thought:  Lighten up, develop the skill of finding humor in tough stuff, and always remember – where there's a will, you'd better get your name on it.

# About the Author

## Anne Barab

Anne Barab, rumored to be the lost love child of Mark Twain and Lucille Ball, is an expert who speaks to people about balancing attitude, reality and behavior to craft lives of significance. Her core message helps people learn how to become more resilient by laughing about the bad stuff as soon as possible.

Anne was COO of a $1.4 billion mortgage bank and served three terms as an elected official.

However, her greatest claim to fame is being married for thirty-four lo-o-ong years to the same engineer, having three children who are not currently in jail, and being voted Best Smelling Mom by her son's first grade.

## Contact Information:

Anne Barab
Barab Associates, Inc.
Dallas, Texas
Phone: (877) 349-2777
www.AnneBarab.com

# What's So Funny?
# Lots of stuff, if we can overcome our fear of having fun.

**By Craig Zablocki**

Someone once said, "Your actions speak so loudly, I cannot hear what you say."

I'd like to devote this chapter to what we consider to be humor in today's society and how we model it. How do our actions affect the people around us? How seriously do we take ourselves? How does that lead to others taking things personally? Can we appear foolish? Do we belittle or lift people up with our humor? Do we use up too much energy trying not to be embarrassed? Why so many damn questions?

Several years ago, my toddler and I were the last ones to board a plane from Minneapolis to Denver. We were assigned seat 4B, the middle seat. Charles was traveling free as a "lap-sitter." To our right sat Mr. Businessman #1; to our left was Mr. Businessman #2.

We had spent the previous night with my cousin and his son, who are really into organic food. Moments before boarding, Charles downed 10 ounces of organic cranberry juice and a multi-nut-whole-grain muffin. As soon as we hit the runway, the juice took effect and Charles did a number two. Within seconds came the second wave: cranberry-colored spit-up all over my white shirt.

I looked at both businessmen and said, "Wonder what's in store for the next hour and 58 minutes?"

Two guys, two totally different responses:

Serious business guy, who probably didn't have kids, or if he did probably controlled the hell out of them, began frowning and grimacing and acting all exasperated.

Fun business guy handed me a napkin, joked about what had happened, and ended up playing with Charles for half the flight.

It's always interesting to see the controlling

types get all uptight when silliness breaks out. Could we possibly model by our actions that we are *not* the center of the universe? Could we let go of the need to control everything?

## Laughter annihilates the ego, and the ego can be a pain in the ass

Recently, I spoke to "teachers of teachers" at the National Teacher Educators Association conference in Chicago. Keep in mind these are the teachers who teach the teachers who teach the kids of America.

I began with a simple activity. I told them to lift their right hand and hold out three fingers. Then I told them to take those three fingers and place them on their chin. I raised three fingers, too, but placed mine on my cheek. Inevitably, 95 percent of the audience put their fingers on their cheek -- not their chin.

Simple activity. Simple point. They did what I *did*, not what I *said*.

After a few minutes I asked, "How many of you can paint a picture?" I looked around the room of 1,300 professors and saw about 30 hands up. Then I asked, "How about singing? How many of you can sing?" About 10 hands went up. Then I asked how many folks in the room had Ph.D.s. Most of the hands went up.

"If I walked in to any kindergarten classroom in the country and asked the children about painting and singing, how many hands would go up?"

"All of them," they agreed.

"So what's up with that?" I asked the teachers of teachers of children.

What is it we are so afraid of? Could it be the judgment of others? If we didn't care what people thought of our paintings or our singing, maybe we'd be singing and painting every day.

As first and second graders we _all_ knew we could paint and sing, but of this large group of education professors only about 3 percent believed they could. Very interesting, especially when we realize that children learn by _what we do_. I went on to ask: "When was the last time you laughed, meatloaf flying out of your mouth, in front of a group of high school students? Or when was the last time you shed tears of sorrow in front of them? When was the last time you asked any of them for help?"

By our actions, we are teaching kids that the norm is to not ask for help and to not cry. The end result: We take ourselves too seriously.

No wonder the LPD (laughs per day) quotient drops as we grow up. Being cool, being right, having our "stuff" together becomes more important than authenticity, fun, and joy.

And remember: Don't tell others to do something you're unwilling to do. The awesome leader Mahatma Gandhi once was asked by a woman in his village to tell her son to stop eating sugar. Gandhi only said, "I'll be back in two weeks."

Two weeks later, Gandhi returned to the woman's home, went to the child and said, "Stop eating sugar." The curious woman asked, "Why did you wait two weeks to tell my son to stop eating sugar when it would have been just as easy two weeks ago?"

Gandhi replied, "Two weeks ago I was eating sugar."

## Being Embarrassed Isn't So Bad At All

What about the fear of embarrassment? The other day in a workshop, I asked a woman to come up and help me with an activity. "No way," she protested, "I will not be embarrassed!" "That's all right," I told her, "You don't have to do anything you don't want to do." Then I thought to myself, "What if instead of living life avoiding embarrassment, we made it OK?"

Do you realize how much energy it takes walking around "trying not to be embarrassed"? "Do I look all right?" "Is there something on my nose?" "What does Sara think of me?" "I hope I don't fall." All of our efforts to "keep it together" lead to a controlling nature that causes us to sometimes think we're about ready to combust. Using so much energy to uphold a serious image keeps us pretty busy — and pretty stressed. What if we made it OK to be embarrassed? We would show kids that we can be silly, make mistakes, and not care so much what people think of us.

If you've ever seen 4-year-olds playing soccer, you'll agree it's a hoot. It's like swarm ball — a bunch of bees swarming around the field, chasing a ball. Who's on offense? Who's on defense? Who cares! They certainly don't.

One day, 4-year-old Michael was in the middle of the field. All of a sudden he stopped, while the rest of the swarm continued. His dad, sitting on the sideline, became concerned. Was he hurt? Suddenly, oblivious to everyone around him, Mike's arms started to swing back and forth. With a big smile on his face, he exclaimed, "I love this game!" Precious.

How many of us walk into our offices on Monday morning and exclaim, with arms extended, "I love this job!" What keeps us from this freedom that is available to us? Think about it. Did Mike stop, hesitate, and think to himself, "I feel like expressing some spontaneous joy, but what will Dad and his friends think of me?" No. He totally didn't care what others thought of him, and in that way he was *free*. And are we not attracted to people who are authentic, who are truly expressive and joyful like Mike?

I can hear what you're thinking: "It's OK for kids, but it's different for adults; what would others think?" I don't know about you, but it was a delight to be in the presence of my grandmother singing Hawaiian songs as we played Scrabble. It was a total crack-up when my father, my son, and I each put two grapes in our upper lips and tried talking to each other without laughing. It was one of the greatest plane trips ever the time a friend and I had all the passengers singing *Row, Row, Row Your Boat*. I love the spontaneous ovations at the fast-food restaurants and watching parents laughing with their kids. Somehow, when one or two of us can let our guard down and risk being foolish, it gives others permission to join in and do the same.

This concept rings clear to me when I ask an audience how many of them have 4- to 7-year-olds at home. "How many of these little ones woke up this morning thinking there was something wrong with them?" I ask. No hands go up. Kids at that age, assuming they have a safe home environment and conscientious parents, don't wake up thinking there is anything wrong with them. Then I ask: "How many of you woke up this morning realizing there is nothing wrong with you?" Usually a few hands go up. About 1 percent of adults wake up thinking they are complete the way they are. The rest of us, well, you know.

## Let's Show 'Em We're OK, So They'll Be OK

Wow, so we're demonstrating that we are not OK with who we are. Then we watch our kids grow up believing the lie that something is wrong with them. I see it in high school kids who take themselves so seriously that they develop significant disorders, but I cannot blame them because we adults have modeled those behaviors for them.

In a study at the University of California, Berkeley, researchers wanted to find out how many times different groups of people laughed each day. They differentiated between race, gender, age, etc. They found that the average 4-year-old laughs 400 times a day, while the average adult laughs seven times. Now there's a discrepancy!

I love this other study about the repression of tears; if we repress tears from laughter or sorrow, we experience rage and aggression. When I work with what I consider "macho groups," like the military, police, or gangs, my job is to get them to simply laugh — to let down their tough images and take themselves lightly. For some men it is a struggle. They were taught growing up that it's not OK to laugh or cry. It was modeled to them that they should act tough.

## A Healthy Sense of Humor Means Just Having Fun

Unfortunately, there is a lot of sick "humor" in our society. Offensive stand-up comics target audience members for personal annihilation.

Sexually explicit and sarcastic sitcoms leave dysfunctional examples for our children. Dark and violent TV shows and movies presented under the guise of humor teach violent, bullying behavior that begins with teasing and "poking fun."

But if you look at the clean humor of Bill Cosby; the silliness and sincerity of Patch Adams; the sweetness, humility, and laughter of the Dali Lama of Tibet; the silly antics of Lucille Ball, we can get an idea of some positive role models.

One of the components of people who model healthy humor and lightheartedness is a fun disposition. When I teach improvisation, I tell people to skip trying to be funny and instead just have fun. When we're having fun, humor and laughter are usually the byproduct.

Remember Bob Dole's run for the presidency? He came across as stern and serious. The night after he lost to Bill Clinton, he was on *The Tonight Show*, where his demeanor was carefree, laid back, and funny. It was a side of Bob Dole that I barely saw during the campaign, and I couldn't help but think how his sense of humor could have helped him in the election.

# How Two Men Rose Above Their Raising

On a plane, a middle-aged man across from me was reading a book. After a time, he closed his book, held it tight, and began quietly crying. I imagine something moved him in the story, or it reminded him of something sorrowful (hell, I have no clue why he was crying; the point is it doesn't matter why he was crying). He just allowed the tears to come, and it was cool. He was totally comfortable with his tears.

On another trip, from Reno to Denver, I was sitting next to a sophisticated man from Washington, D.C. He was employed at the State Department and had several hundred people working for him. We began chatting, and before long we were engaged in a philosophical discussion about human conditioning, like why we don't laugh.

Just days before, on my birthday, I had received a plastic booger as a gag gift. There was an expandable part that swelled up in the nostril, and it looked pretty realistic — and really gross, too. So halfway into the flight we had talked about this stuff enough. He was talking about the old days, and how he and his wife had more fun and took more chances. While he was strolling down memory lane, I nonchalantly reached into my bag, concealing the little prop in my hand. I faked a sneeze, and as I released my hands from my nose, there it was — dangling. At first he freaked, especially as I leaned toward him looking for help. He reached for his napkin to help me out and finally realized it was a joke. He was laughing so hard. I said "We've been talking about how you need to take yourself less seriously — to lighten up a bit more. Now is when we stop talking and take some action."

I left for the restroom to wash it. When I returned, I offered my new friend the challenge: "If you sit here with this in your nose and we talk with the flight attendants, you'll make my day. If you put this in your nose and with a straight face walk down the length of this plane, you'll make my week."

"I can't do it," he objected.

"Yes you can," I reassured him.

"No," he protested again.

"It's now or never — it's time to get your life back," I said, exaggerating a bit. "I'll support you."

"Give it to me."

He took the piece of rubber, put it in his nose, adjusted his tie, stood up, and with a straight face walked the entire length of the plane. I followed a few yards behind and, granted, most people were busy reading or sleeping, but the people who did look up had some surprised expressions. When we got back to our seats, my friend was lit up!

As I got off the plane in Denver he asked, "Can I have this puppy?"

"You bet," I said. "Who's picking you up in D.C.?"

"My wife," he said with a mischievous smile.

I handed him my card and told him he had to let me know what happened.

The next day he left me a message saying how much fun he had on his next flight and that he used the gag as he said goodbye to the flight attendants as he left the plane. He wore it all the way to the baggage claim, where he was planning to meet his wife. He said her jaw dropped, then they both cracked up laughing.

I have received calls from this man over the years, and he shares with me all the cool things he and his wife have done — dance lessons, fun vacations; he even tried out for a play. A 3-inch piece of rubber was all he needed to get back to the place of having fun and not taking himself too seriously. The difference for this man was putting into action what most people only talk about. And what a great example he was to the rest of us.

# About the Author
## Craig J. Zablocki

A nationally known speaker and consultant, Craig has shared the platform with President George W. Bush, Tom Peters, and Al Gore. Craig presents to Fortune 500 companies, legislators, public service and healthcare professionals, college students, non-profit service organizations, and victims' rights groups. He was the first outside speaker to address the student body of Columbine High School after its tragedy.

Craig inspires audience members to see life in a different way and to take action that brings positive results. One participant even wrote, "We should try to harness Craig's energy—it could power a small city. His passion and commitment are contagious!"

## Contact Information:

Craig Zablocki
634 Marion St. • Denver, CO 80218
Phone: (303) 830-7996
Fax: (303) 830-0194
E-mail: craig@PositivelyHumor.com
www.PositivelyHumor.com

# The Experience of a Lifetime: Humor and Marriage

**By Tim and Kris O'Shea**

Marriage is no joke, so when you find ways to communicate and have fun, it's a real pleasure. For some, working with their spouse could be a challenge. The constant stress, nagging, and whining — and that's just from the husband.

Fortunately, as a husband and wife performing team, we have built a solid foundation that helps us to work well together. We began our relationship as co-performers onstage, and over the years we've learned some valuable principles about how to support one another, think creatively, and, most important, have fun. These principles enable us to both *like* — and *want* — to be around each other.

"Yeah, right," we hear you saying. Fair enough. Read on.

Our journey began with several ventures, including comedy writing, sketch work, stand-up comedy, and improvisation. As humor experts, we apply many of these techniques to our work, marriage, and daily lives. Does that mean we never argue? Of course not. But most of the time, we laugh and have a positively fantastic-fun time.

Whenever we tell people we work together, they say, "I could never do that" or "Is it scary?" or more frequently, "Are you nuts?" They usually add, "Sure, you can do it, but what about the average Joe? My partner and I could never make it work."

But that is simply not true. An awareness of these skills can help you to maintain, enhance, or even transform areas of your life, including your personal relationships.

## Use "Yes, and . . ."

In our careers, we have found that the skill of improvising has the most crossover into other areas of our lives, both professional and personal.

Improvisation has been around a long time, but recently it has become popularized by the television show *Whose Line Is It Anyway?* Essentially, improvisation is people working together to make up a scene spontaneously, based on a suggestion solicited from the audience. It is not stand-up comedy, where one person is telling mostly scripted jokes. Nor is it sketch comedy, which is a group of people performing scripted scenes, such as on *Saturday Night Live.*

A major concept in improvisation is called "Yes, and." Put simply, it is accepting any and every idea that is put before you, then building upon those ideas with your own. For example, when an actor says to you onstage, "I'm a pilot," the scene flows better if you say, "Yes you are a pilot, and...." To say something such as "No you're not, you're a fish" can kill the momentum of the scene.

Are there times with your spouse that you feel like you keep hitting a brick wall? (Or as if you have been hitting your own head against a wall, repeatedly, without access to aspirin or an icepack?) When this happens, you may be in "No, but" mode. This mode is so common that most people don't even know they are doing it. Yet "No, but," is what puts most people in divorce court. Or worse, in *People's Court.*

Think about it: At first, you and your spouse are in that lovey-dovey, can't-get-enough-of-you, whatever-you-say-is-wonderful mode. You're in the land of "yes, and." Once you settle in, however, the little disagreements begin. Suddenly, the person you love to be around is also grating on your last nerve. You can't agree on where to eat, how to raise the kids, or if you should spend your vacation in Maui or Tulsa (well, that last one is a bit easier to decide). In essence, a whole lotta "no's" and "but's."

The remedy? Adopt a little "yes, and" into your lives. Try this simple game, which can be played while driving, making dinner, standing in line at Home Depot, riding a tandem bicycle, or anywhere you might be interacting with each other.

- One person makes a simple statement such as, "Let's go for a walk."
- The other person responds with, "Yes, and...," and adds his own idea about the walk.
- The first person responds with "Yes, and..." and adds her own idea.
- They go back and forth, beginning each sentence with the words "Yes, and."

Play this game with your spouse, and you will find

yourself laughing and getting back into that spontaneous, playful place of possibilities again.

We had a group of managers use this exercise as a way to improve communication with employees. When we followed up a month later, one manager told us that "Yes, and" worked in her personal life, too. Her husband, who was unaware of the concept, didn't know what to make of it when she used it on him. Pretty soon, she told us, he had agreed to a vacation in Barbados and a spa treatment. The power of "Yes, and!"

Warning: Don't do this with a credit card within reach.

## Make it about the other person

So much of what everyone does in life is about getting his/her own needs met. It's easy to get into "I need" mode. And why not? You are with yourself 24 hours a day. When you get down to it, at the basic level, all you have is you.

But what if you are married? Now you have you, plus another. Suddenly you have to balance your needs with the needs of another person. How can you give your partner what he/she needs and let that person know what you need?

There's a concept in theatrical acting that says: "Make your partner look good, and you will look good." This is true onstage, in relationships, in business, and in life. We're not saying that you shouldn't allow yourself to get what you need. We're saying that if each member of the relationship gives the other person what he/she needs — makes it about the other person — then everyone is happy.

In our business, we have found that our most successful programs are the ones where we make it all about the people in the audience. The positive reaction comes from people hearing material that we've written about the company or in seeing one of their own featured onstage. They love it.

And so does your spouse. She loves it when you make it all about her. He loves it when you treat him like it's his birthday, even when it isn't.

Think of your last birthday, or any other occasion where you received a gift. Have you ever gotten a gift that was more for the person giving it than for you? Remember how you felt? You were disappointed in the gift PLUS you had to pretend you appreciated it. (It's a bit like when you were single and your friends would set you up on a blind date — it was frustrating to realize that your friends thought that Jabba the Hut was a perfect match for you.)

On the other hand, when you get a gift that totally fits your personality, or is exactly what you wanted, it's a different feeling, right? You are much happier, more excited, and you really feel that the other person knows you well. You feel like the person really cares about you.

When you focus your attention away from yourself and onto the other person, it makes a huge difference. Dale Carnegie pointed out that a person's name is his or her favorite sound in the whole world. And it is also true that a person's favorite subject is themselves. Is your spouse *your* favorite subject? How can you make sure you are making your relationship about your partner? How can you be there for him/her? What can you do to make that special someone feel like it's his/her birthday today, even if it isn't? ("Wow! A check for 10 grand! How did you know?")

## Enjoy your life together — now

We've all done it. We often continue to do it. We say to ourselves, "I'll be happy when ..."

It is so easy to put off our happiness until tomorrow — after we get done what we think we need to accomplish in order to be happy. We tend to think that we will be happy once we're on vacation, once the kids are grown, once the house is clean, once he stops being a jerk, once she stops whining, once we have a new house, once we can afford to paint the new house, once we've landscaped, once we've paid off the car. At this rate, we'll be happy when we are dead.

When improvising onstage or in life, it is essential to be in the moment. The moment is where the possibilities and fun live. When we are future-tripping or past-grabbing, we are not available to really connect with what's important.

If you don't enjoy your life right now, you're not going to enjoy it once you've gotten that item on your "to do" list accomplished — because inevitably, there will be something else that you will need to accomplish in order to be happy, and you're right back to where you started.

Don't wait. Enjoy the moment. Have fun in your marriage — now! Happiness happens now. Love happens now. When you started dating, did you say, "I'll love you once we get married"? No. You allowed yourself to be happy, have fun, and enjoy that moment.

Recently, we had an important business trip to Dallas that was occupying all of our attention. We were spending so much time getting ready that anytime we needed to do something else, it was prefaced with "after Dallas." It became a running joke. "I'll enjoy my dinner...after Dallas." "I'll take a shower...after Dallas."

What is your Dallas? How can you return to the moment? What can you do now to reconnect to your relationship? Remember, if you can't have fun and enjoy your life now, then what's the point?

## Applause, applause

Marriage is about having fun, enjoying each other's company, and treasuring your travels through life together. And life is short, so have fun now. Live together, love together, and above all, laugh together (just don't laugh when your spouse is naked).

When we practice these principles, we are part of a magical experience in which we connect with something greater than ourselves. Creating a space of possibilities, connecting with your partner, and finding the fun in the moment gives rise to thunderous applause and joy. So tonight, when your partner gets home, rise to your feet and give him, or her, a standing ovation!

*"A successful marriage requires falling in love many times, always with the same person." —Mignon McLaughlin*

# About the Author

## Tim and Kris O'Shea

Described as "absolutely hilarious" by audiences across the country, Kris's on-stage expertise has grown from a broad spectrum of experience. Kris found herself working as a corporate entertainer in 1991, while earning her degree in theater. Her professional experience as a sales consultant and corporate trainer have given her the edge to understand what goes on in the workplace...and why it's funny!

Tim has been a humor writer and performer for radio, stage, and corporate video productions since 1990. Tim honed his comedic skills in sketch and improvisation, and spent 12 years on the stand-up circuit. He has also worked in several Fortune 500 venues in sales, management, and human resources, which made him all too familiar with the common office obstacles. Combining business sense with performance talent, Tim has found a natural fit making corporate audiences laugh.

## Contact Information:

Tim and Kris O'Shea
Experience Productions • Westminster, CO
Phone: 303-371-2849
www.ExperienceProductions.net

# Got Magic? Don't pull disasters out of thin air; use your powers to see what's really there

**By Brad Barton**

My young friend Heidi went to a department store to buy the polyester pants required for her new job. She tried a pair on and stood in front of the three-way mirror. To her horror, she realized the pants made her look *fat*.

Heidi really needed the job, so she reluctantly took the pants to the sales counter. It was mid-December. The store was bustling with Christmas shoppers. She had to wait in line for an excruciating 20 minutes, all the while revisiting the image of herself in the mirror. "I'm fat, I'm fat," was all she could think.

To make matters worse, she could see she was about to be waited on by a cute sales clerk. When the clerk turned from the register to serve Heidi, he looked at her apologetically, leaned forward, and said, "I am so sorry about your *weight*."

Heidi, too stunned to be angry, burst into tears and ran sobbing from the store. Halfway home, still in tears, she realized what the sales clerk had meant. The frazzled clerk really did feel bad. The store had not hired enough Christmas help. He was not criticizing her **weight** but was apologizing for her 20-minute **wait!**

## YOUR VERY OWN 'APPEARING' ACT

Have you ever created a disaster out of nothing but misguided anticipation or interpretation? Perhaps you have taken offense at a co-worker's comment, worked it up in your mind to the level of an in-office Hiroshima, and later discovered its innocent intent. Or maybe you have negatively interpreted a word or a look from your spouse and reacted emotionally, your misguided response creating the very conflict you anticipated.

Isn't it true that many of our negative experiences and feelings are of our own making? Our perceptions and interpretations powerfully influence our responses and reactions, and sometimes they create the very thing we fear.

You see what amazing wizards we are? We have the power to create magical results or illusions of disaster out of nothing more than our intent and interpretation. But if our interpretation and perception can create the illusion of disaster, can the same power create the magic of beauty, opportunity, and even great humor out of an apparent misfortune?

Monitoring our perceptions and actively cultivating our ability to choose our interpretations powerfully and positively impact our quality of life. We literally change our lives -- like magic! Anais Nin said, "People don't live life as it is, they live life as they are" -- as they perceive it through the filters of their interpretations based on their attitudes and expectations.

## A 5-YEAR-OLD MAGIC WAND

Several years ago, I was having a crash-and-burn day. Nothing had gone right, and I came home frustrated, crabby, and annoyed. (Of course, you never have days like that, right?) I realized that if I stayed upstairs with my family I was going to infect them all with my negativity. Attitudes are, after all, contagious, right? So I made the noble choice to remove myself to my downstairs office.

OK, I'll be honest. Actually, my wife sternly ordered, "Get downstairs, Brad! We are getting sick of your attitude!"

I grumbled my way downstairs. After about 15 minutes of feeling utterly sorry for myself, I heard the pitter-patter of little feet. I looked over my shoulder to see my five-year-old, Jacob, negotiating his way down the steep staircase.

"Jacob, get back upstairs," I growled. "Dad is not in the mood to talk to you right now." Like I said, I was in a pretty nasty mood. But Jacob didn't hesitate. He trotted up to me and said emphatically, "Dad, I *gotta* talk to you."

That's when I noticed that Jacob had a cold – a really messy cold, with green and yellow stuff running out of his nose and kinda smeared on his face. As he sputtered excitedly about whatever it was he just *had* to tell me, that icky nose stuff got worse. I looked at him in utter disgust, thinking, "Whose kid is *this*?"

Did I mention I was not in a good mood?

"Daaa-a-d," he insisted, "It's really, really 'portant. I gotta talk to you!"

I put down my pen, swiveled my chair toward him, leaned over, and said, "What!"

My messy little 5-year-old stretched up on his tip-toes, grabbed me by the ears in a death grip, and pulled my face to within an inch of his own. He quickly licked my right eye and then my left eye, exclaimed "I love you Dad!" then took off running.

Now *I* had slimy snot all over *my* face. (Did I mention I was already in a very foul mood?)

Jacob raced back up the stairs, yelling, "Momma! I did just what you told me! I licked Dad right in the eyes and said, 'I love you!' "

What? *She* was in on this? I was already furious at Jacob, now *two* people were in trouble!

I heard my wife's incredulous response: "You did *what?* I told you to go downstairs and *look* your dad in the eyes and tell him you love him."

I stumbled to the bathroom. As I washed the virus-ridden mucous from my eyes, I began to laugh – really laugh. Have you ever laughed so hard that your gut aches? It hurts, but doesn't it feel great? Extra oxygen flows to the brain, endorphins flow – and perceptions change *like magic!*

I dried my face and walked upstairs in a completely changed mood. I went looking for my little Jacob, who had retreated into hiding when he realized his blunder. I picked him up and hugged him. Like 5-year-olds do, he wrapped all four limbs around me and hugged me back. The feeling of love and gratitude that swept through me was pure magic. I stood there in awe, realizing what a wonderful gift I had received. I thought to myself, "No matter how grown up this little boy gets – maybe with a son of his own someday – from this night on he will always be my very own little Jacob-man who, on a very bad day, 'licked me in the eyes' and told me he loved me – and magically changed my perception *and my reality.*" This bad thing was really a good thing, a very good thing. It is now a cherished memory, mucus and all. That is the magic power of intention and perception.

And then, about 48 hours later, I came down with a really nasty cold. I had three days at home in bed to consider how licky, uh, I mean *lucky*, I truly am.

## The Power Within

Stephen Covey says it this way: "It isn't what happens to us that affects our behavior. It is our interpretation of what happens to us. And when we can learn to get a better paradigm, get to a different level of thinking, then we are on the road to significant improvement." Covey calls this the essence of self-determination.

I call it magic.

Real magic is the ability to change your perception and thereby alter your experience – your reality. To turn a bad deal into a good deal simply by changing the way you look at it – that is powerful magic. In this particular case, I didn't intentionally choose my new perception; life handed it to me as a gift, and I accepted it. Think about it. If life has the power to do this serendipitously, isn't it possible for you and I to perform this trick on purpose? When we do, we've truly "Got Magic."

When I was 8 years old, my grandmother came to live with us. As a young woman, Grandma Sessions immigrated to the United States from South Africa. She retained a rich South African accent throughout her life. In her very old age she suffered from chronic headaches. Loud noises, like my eight rambunctious brothers and sisters and me wrestling and fighting, made her headaches even worse. She especially hated our music. She called rock 'n roll "that damnable boom, boom, boom!"

Grandma had been with us eight years when my sister Julie and her 3-year old son, Jason, came home to live with us. Jason was cute, but he was spoiled rotten. When he didn't get his way (which was often), he'd throw himself on the floor, flailing his arms and legs and exuding high-pitched screams. These outbursts would send Grandma's headaches clean off the pain chart. After months of mounting tension, my grandmother finally exploded. She screamed at my mother at the top of her frail lungs, "Maaa-a-a-ry, get in here!" Mother rushed in to find

Grandma in her favorite yellow chair, beet-red with anger. In her elegant South African accent she yelled, "I can't stand it any longer! This house is too small for the both of us. One of us has got to go; it's me or that boy."

Mother calmly walked to the adjoining bathroom and began to run water into the tub. She then walked back and calmly asked, "Mother, would you like a little bit of water or a lot of water in the tub?"

My confused grandmother stared at her, then countered, "What do you mean? You gave me a bath this morning!"

Mother explained, "Jason is little, and to get rid of him only takes a little water. If we are going to get rid of you, we'll need the whole tub full. Your choice." They stared at each other for a few tense seconds, then burst into laughter. They really laughed – hard. They laughed until they thought their sides would split. Then they laughed some more. Grandma's frustration – and her headache – disappeared, at least for the moment.

## POOF! A DAZZLING NEW YOU

Comedian Michael Pritchard said, "Laughter is a bit like changing a baby's diaper. It doesn't fix the problem permanently, but it makes everything OK – for a little while." The facts at the Barton home hadn't changed – but perceptions had. Jason's outbursts still caused Grandmother pain, but in one good 15-minute belly laugh, a whole summer of stress and anxiety was swept away.

When things got really bad after that, Grandmother would just yell, "Maaa-a-ry, fill the bath *all* the way. I am ready to go now!"

As a professional speaker, author, and magician, I have the privilege and power to change perceptions in the minds of audiences all around the world. I use the metaphor of magic and illusion to challenge old beliefs and perceptions, create new insights, and empower corporations and educators. It's great fun to dazzle a crowd with impossible feats of magic on stage, but there is greater power in each of us to shift reality through the power of intent, perception, and interpretation.

In seemingly insignificant moments, our reactive perceptions shape our interpretations, those interpretations guide our decisions, and those decisions ultimately create our quality of life.

The power lies within us to transform negative perceptions – destructive illusions of reality – through positive, constructive interpretations. When we can give circumstances like getting "licked in the eyes" the best possible interpretation, we magically create a new reality. We transform tragedy into opportunity, create really good days from really bad days, and "poof," a better life appears – just like magic!

Got Magic? Yes, you do.

# About the Author

## Brad Barton

Are you having a tough day? Is your business going through a narrow passage? Brad will have you believing in your own magic before you can say "Shazaam"! Corporate leaders and professional educators love Brad's humorous and inspiring messages drawn from his life experiences on a cattle ranch with 8 siblings, a colorful grandmother, a learning disability, and an unbelievable mentor.

Within the tales and tricks of this high energy keynote speaker lies a deeper message. Join satisfied clients Kimberly-Clark, US Dep't of Defense, NCAA, Autoliv, IRS, and Kroger Foods, in discovering that we each have serious magic – inner power that helps us overcome destructive illusions and discover the greatness in ourselves and those around us.

Brad's best trick is not an illusion; it is revealing that You've Got Magic!

## Contact Information:

Brad Barton
Brad Barton Communications, Inc.
Ogden, UT
Phone: (888) GOT-MAGIC
(468-6244)
Brad@BradBartonSpeaks.com
www.BradBartonSpeaks.com

# Don't Just Talk About It... *Use* Humor!
# Humor in Action
## by Michael Aronin

When Brad called to ask if I wanted to be a part of *Humor Us*, I knew the answer would be yes because working with him on our first effort, *Humor Me*, had been a breeze. Maybe he just made it look easy. The other reason was the highly favorable feedback I've received from the book.

In *Humor Me*, I dealt mainly with my own history, how having cerebral palsy shaped my sense of humor, and how my sense of humor shaped having cerebral palsy. For *Humor Us* I'm taking a different tack, and pointing out the value added in living life with humor, and of actually using humor every day – particularly on those days when it might be easier to react with an acidic insult or those times when our fear of the new or unknown is trying to block us from jumping in feet-first.

Some of the following stories involve me; some do not. But the common thread they all share is that they involve people who consciously *chose* to view a situation in a more lighthearted fashion, and by doing so, either diffused a tense situation, cleared the brambles of fear from the path to the unknown, or simply created a memory worth laughing at even years later. So here we go with a quick ticking down of some examples of the power of humor in real life. Humor in the trenches, humor in action.

## Fakin' It, not Really Makin' It

When *Humor Me* came out in October 2003, I gave some copies to family and friends. One of these friends was Cathy. One day in December, we were discussing our plans for New Year's Eve. I was to be performing stand-up comedy and she was to be playing keyboard for a local band.

"That's great," I said. "I didn't know you played keyboard." She said she didn't, but that she and her boyfriend, who frequently go dancing, had become friendly with this band whose keyboard player had suddenly quit. One night, the lead singer approached her and explained the band's predicament. He asked if she would play keyboard for them the following week through New Year's Eve. He assured her that she didn't have to know *how* to play since their keyboard music was pre-recorded. All Cathy would have to do was stand behind the keyboard and *pretend* she was doing something – a little like an employee of the Department of Motor Vehicles. The only difference was that she needed a positive attitude to do this job.

The band was at a club five minutes from my house on New Year's, so I stopped by after finishing at the Improv. Watching her, I giggled to myself that I was one of just a few people in the room who knew what was really going on.

But what took me most by *surprise*, was just *why*

she agreed to do it in the first place. The band asked her to do this right after she'd read Mark Mayfield's chapter in *Humor Me* in which he writes about finding more humor by jumping in and trying different experiences. Cathy was most influenced when Mark talked about the ability to laugh at yourself, which she did, over and over during her days with the band.

## A Call from that Special Someone

In my case, CP affects my speech and motor skills. I walk and talk slowly, my hands shake, and I drag my left foot. In the spirit of these "slight" affectations, my keynote speech is entitled, *"Walking the Talk . . . Well Kind Of."* In it, I talk about the power of humor. But I also try to walk the talk when I'm *not* on the speaker's platform, especially when I think I can ease the discomfort others sometimes feel in my presence.

Several days before a speech at a teachers' in-service meeting, I began working with the head of their art department (I'll call her Mrs. Smith), to select staff photos I'd be using as overheads. I called Mrs. Smith at home and her husband answered. Jumping to conclusions based on the sound of my voice, he shouted, "Honey, it's for you! I think it's someone from the Special Olympics!"

Mrs. Smith got on the phone and I acted as though nothing was amiss. But when I saw her at the presentation, I could tell she was embarrassed. When she started to apologize, I chimed in and said, "Don't feel bad. Your husband gave me a great idea. Since that call to you, I've raised $8,000.00. And I might *give* some of that to the Special Olympics!"

## nuts? Putts.

I love people who can make me laugh. My friend, Jon Putt can do this. Jon and I were at an amusement park one day, when out of nowhere, he pointed to my crotch and screamed, "The guy's nuts, grab 'em!"

Now, the fact that these words were screamed at the top of his lungs, and that it was impossible for passersby to determine whether he meant "grab them" or "grab him," didn't matter. What *did* matter was that it was crazy and funny and I didn't expect it. I laughed for five minutes with tears of laughter streaming down my face.

He got me again not long ago when I called him

for the phone number of someone we know. He rattled off a number and I thanked him before rushing off the phone. It was one of those days when I was trying to do ten things at once. I began to dial: 4-1-0-6-7-2 . . . "Hey wait a second," I thought, "This is *my* number!" I called him back, and when he picked up, all I heard was laughing on the other end.

And since the nut doesn't fall far from the tree, his father, Ken reached over and tickled my wife one day in a fabric store when she bumped into him and mentioned that she'd come there to get felt. Think about it.

## Ding-Dong Calling

A few years ago my mother-in-law bought a new phone. She called and asked me to call her right back so she could make sure it worked. If you ever met my mother-in-law, you would want to slap me for even *thinking* about teasing her. She happens to be the best mother-in-law I could have ever asked for, and is incredibly easy-going. I said, "Sure, Mom," then hung up and didn't call her back. She waited about two minutes, then called me again. I said, "Mom, what happened? I called and it rang and rang and rang."

She said, "Let's try again." We hung up. Again, I failed to call her. She called back in another two minutes, but this time when I picked up, she said, "Put your wife on the phone."

## Humor in Traction

My grandfather, who was 90 at the time, was in the hospital for a few days, flat on his back. After adjusting his bed, the nurse asked, "Mr. Rosenthal, are you comfortable?"

"I make a good living," he said.

## Pinkie Swearing

Another close friend of mine is a comic named Hood. About five years ago, we were booked at a college in upstate New York. On the trip up, we ran into a snowstorm that got worse by the minute. I borrowed Hood's cell phone to call my wife, Teece. (By the way, Teece was referred to as Patricia, her given name, in *Humor Me*, so I have not run through yet another wife.) She answered, but then quickly faded out. Hood said, "Give me the phone." He said, "Hi, Teece. Yeah. Hold on." He handed the phone back, and I said, "Hello, Teece?" No Teece, so Hood grabbed the phone from me again and said, "Teece, yeah. Hold on. Michael's a moron." He handed the phone back to me. "Hello, Teece?" Nothing! Hood then told me to hold the phone with two fingers. I did. Nothing happened. Then he said for me to hold it with my pinkie up. I did that too and still nothing happened – except for the slowly dawning realization that Teece had never been there since that time when she'd first faded out.

## A Relationship on the Rocks

At a time when I had fallen in love with Teece, but her feelings still teetered between friendship and romance, I landed a stand-up gig in Hilton Head and cleverly asked her to go along. We had a nice suite with a kitchenette and plenty of space for Teece to escape to - all part of my sneaky plan to make her think she was safe. Knowing that Teece loves Amaretto, I scored big points when I pulled a surprise bottle out of my luggage. "Oh that was so sweet of you!" she cooed, and I laughed an evil laugh inside my mind.

Later, Teece was in the bathroom putting on her

makeup before dinner. She'd reached that point where she really didn't notice the Cerebral Palsy anymore and had started to forget that some tasks were better left to her. She leaned toward the bathroom door and called, "If you're all ready, would you mind refilling the ice cube trays? We'll need them later for the Amaretto."

"Sure," I said. "And before you come out, would you mind making sure you're a blonde first?"

You know, a clever come-back *can* shoot you in the foot. But I couldn't stop myself. Thank God Teece laughed, and she laughed so hard that she realized right exactly then that she had fallen in love with me.

## Cruising for a Bruising

My grandfather (the comfortable one) decided to take the family on a cruise to Nova Scotia. On the morning of the trip, as we gathered excitedly at my mother's house, I gave Mom a big hug and inadvertently fractured one of her ribs.

"You broke Mommy," my sister said with a gasp. The words made us laugh even harder -- even Mom. When we boarded the ship later that day (a total of eight, including my grandfather, his caregiver, my 1-year-old Sydney, and my stepfather Roy), my mother didn't appear to be in any pain.

This was a time when Teece, a first-time mother, was experiencing friction with Mom over her concern that Teece wasn't getting Syd out of the house enough, that the baby needed to be learning more about the world.

Upon reaching Nova Scotia, we all went ashore. Starting up the road with Mom and Roy pushing Syd in her stroller, we could hear Mom saying things like, "See, Sydney? That's what a horse looks like," and "See, Sydney? That's what a rock looks like."

Then, somehow, they lost their grip on the stroller and Syd began rolling down a steep incline. We all ran to catch her. Faster and faster she went, until the stroller hooked to the right off the sidewalk and started down an embankment. The stroller hit a fence at the bottom, bounced back, and stopped.

Breathing hard, we caught up to her and were relieved to see that she was OK and had even enjoyed the ride.

"See, Sydney?" said Teece, jamming the heel of her hand against her face and not missing a beat. "This is what a chain-link fence looks like."

Laughing about it later, Teece said her intention was not to be sarcastic but to take a difference of opinion and make it something funny. And to their credit, she and Mom began laughing -- until my mother's rib started to hurt and they had to stop.

## He Who Laughs Last

What's my point? The point is that you can study humor as much as you like, but it won't make a difference in your life until you start to implement it. So go ahead and tell a joke. Play a gag on a pal. Laugh at yourself. Don't just read about humor; do it.

So there you have it. That's all I have to say on the subject of choosing humor – until my family, friends, and I have taken a few more cruises and gotten *felt* again.

# About the Author

## Michael Aronin

Michael is a nationally acclaimed speaker who encourages people to improve their skills in the workplace while lifting their spirits and making them smile. Also a skilled comedian, he shows audience members how to get past personal shortcomings and move forward in their careers in entertaining and enlightening ways.

As a physically challenged member of the business community, Michael combines his personal experience with facts to provide a unique perspective on overcoming obstacles that goes far beyond "textbook knowledge."

**Contact Information:**
Michael Aronin
Rising Above
152 Langdon Farm Cr.
Odenton, MD 21113
Phone: (410) 672-2565
www.michaelaronin.com

# The Up Side of Upside-Down Using Humor to Turn Embarrassing Moments Into Treasured Memories

## By Deb Gauldin, RN, PMS

"You must be the comedian they hired," huffed the correctional officer, arms folded sternly across the chest of his starched uniform. "OK, so *make me laugh.*"

Boy, nothing sets a speaker at ease like a warm welcome!

Correctional officers from across the state

of Iowa had gathered for an annual conference, and I was hired to start the day with humor.

It was clearly time to draw upon skills honed from 20-plus years of bedside nursing and teaching Lamaze classes, and over a decade working as a professional humorist. I took a deep cleansing breath and asked myself two questions: What wound is causing this person's attitude, and in what way can humor ease this person's pain?

Well, maybe I was actually thinking, "Why is this guy a jerk, and how am I going to get him to laugh?"

In my experience, negativity usually stems from an underlying fear or pain, a "wounded-ness" if you will. And while I am not in the position to fix or even diagnose the cause, I have witnessed over and over again the powerful balm that laughter is when treating ills of all kinds.

Applied generously and judiciously, laughter has amazing restorative properties. It's the Rx for reducing both physical *and* emotional suffering. Best of all, it's free, and the more you use it, the more accessible it becomes.

So, how did this nurse finally make the "bad cop" laugh? I turned the situation Upside-Down. This is an actual technique used in improvisational theater. I use it to help me see the humor in everyday interactions and also to create comedy and music for keynote presentations. These include original music and parodies written specifically for very different clients and industries. The Upside- Down method helps me do this.

For example, in the case of lyrics, I may be asked to write a song about an unfamiliar subject or product – say, a new device that helps with bladder control, or a software system used in ATMs. Instead of feigning a level of expertise (OK, so I may have a little experience with bladder control), I turn the topic Upside-Down. Instead of writing what I *know*, I flip it, and write about what I *don't know*.

For example, an ATM lyric might be

*When I need cash for my low-fat latte,*
*I don't mean to gripe.*
*Nothing's worse than caffeine withdrawal,*
*When my debit card won't swipe."*

Here's another example. These lyrics are set to the Beatles tune, *"With A Little Help from My Friends."*

*What would you say if my bladder gave way?*
*Would you stand up and walk out on me?*
*Lend me your ear and I'll sing you this song,*
*About bladder incontinency.*

*Oh, I'll get by with a little help from Depends.*
*Oh I'll sit high with a little help from Depends.*

*Do you trickle when you're tickled?*
*Just know you're not alone.*
*Do you dribble when you wiggle?*
*You're just lacking sphincter tone.*

*Maybe it's aging or having some babies.*
*Or maybe it's a genetic tendency.*
*But, this is my story and I'm stickin' to it.*
*It's because "parole officers" are too busy to pee.*

I'm back from the restroom now and back to the point. In the case of the corrections officer, I flipped the conversation Upside-Down so that we were talking about *him:* "What do you find amusing in your line of work? I bet you have a million funny stories. I'd love to hear one."

Soon we are *both* laughing and benefiting from another of laughter's healing properties: its remarkable ability to help us connect with one another. Flipping negativity Upside-Down, results in a positive attitude. It's a choice anyone can make. Do you see an opportunity to try this with someone irritating you?

When my daughter subscribed to teen magazines,

she and her girlfriends would rush in from the mailbox and immediately turn to the "Most embarrassing moments" feature. They gasped in horror and giggled uncontrollably at tales of kisses gone wrong and disastrous hairdos. They weren't laughing *at* the people in the magazines; they were identifying *with* and relating *to* them.

Laughing helped them cope with their own embarrassing moments and fears. After all, if the girls in the magazines had lived through such humiliation, perhaps my daughter and her friends would survive as well. With time, the most embarrassing moments become some of the funniest to recall. Our lives are actually enriched when we take an embarrassing moment and turn it Upside-Down.

## Here's an Upside-Down doozie of my own:

As a child, I enjoyed playing the clarinet but dreaded recital time. For years I was overcome with stage fright. I would hear my name called and tremble onto the stage. When the accompaniment began, I'd play a few unsteady measures, and then simply stop. Stop entirely, until tiny Mrs. Sutton would leave her piano bench and join me on stage. She'd call my name and give me a little shake or two. I would "snap to," dutifully begin again, and finish the song without a hitch. Nonetheless, this experience was terrifying.

Years later, I was invited to sing at a wedding. The soprano I sat next to in choir was getting married. Since she was vocally trained and had very high standards, I was flattered to be asked. I didn't realize she was marrying a boy I once had a major crush on. After all, he played the bagpipes. What a turn on!

After intense rehearsal, I nailed the Karen Carpenter rendition of "Why do birds suddenly appear ..." The second selection was a droning, monotonous tune by Peter, Paul and Mary that contained the phrase "There is love" repeated several hundred times. The lyrics included something about a man cleaving his mother and some troubadors. Go figure. (Or was it leaving his mother? I have a slight tendency to mix up lyrics.)

The blessed day arrived. The butterflies began. The dry mouth and sweaty palms followed. "Birds suddenly appeared," and I made it through the first song. Now my brain was screeching, "Whatever you do, Deb, don't freeze. Don't stop, no matter what. Keep going. Keep going."

The purpose of song two was to set the mood for the lighting of the unity candles. I took a deep breath, vowed once again that I wouldn't stop, and began singing:

> *He is now to be among you at the calling of your hearts.*
>
> *Rest assured this troubador is acting on his part.*
>
> *I used to sit by Candy in choir and did you know*
>
> **(no, this wasn't part of the song!)**
>
> *I went on a few dates with Mickey and he had real nice bagpipes.*
>
> *They probably already packed their suitcases and they are going on a honeymoon  . . .*

Everything that came into my mind came out of my mouth. I couldn't stop!

Several *"There is love..."* refrains later and it was over. Red-faced and sure the bride would never speak to me again, I leapt out of the balcony, bounded down the steps, and flew into the street outside the church. My boyfriend was waiting for me in his re-built Ford Fairlane. "Hit it! Go! Go!" I shrieked.

Unable to see any humor at the time, I didn't tell anyone what had happened. In fact, I was so afraid of what might or might not come out of my mouth, I did not sing in front of others for years. I was afraid to even join in on my favorite Christmas carol, "Jack Frost Roasting on an Open Fire." Or were those chestnuts roasting....?

And what of the bride and groom, you ask? I never saw or heard of them again! That is the honest truth! I don't recall a thank you or even a "How Could You?" note. Of course, I spent a few years wearing a disguise whenever I ventured out in public, and I avoided parades and bagpipes, but never again did our paths cross. So maybe I never really dressed incognito, but in telling this story, even thirty years later, I still shudder. I sell CDs and DVDs, yet fear coming face to face with that 1970's reel to reel tape. Just now, I gave the couple fake names in case either ever read this book. (Like Cindy or Mike wouldn't recognize the situation!)

Are there embarrassing moments in your life that you still carry around? Of course there are. We all have them. The issue becomes whether or not we let those situations define us today. Are regrets or embarrassments from your past keeping you from expressing who you really are? Are they preventing you from moving in the direction of your deepest desires? If so, then turn them around. Turn them Upside-Down.

I spent too many years letting the "wedding incident" convince me I could never trust what may come out of my mouth. That incident could have prevented me from ever taking the risk to sing in public again. It could have prevented me from bringing replenishing laughter and music to hundreds of overextended and underappreciated audiences. I ask you, "If I hadn't flipped things Upside-Down, where would the criminal justice system in Iowa be today?"

Determined to let this incident go, I began singing along with the radio and my children. I created some funny songs and shared them with preschoolers. Still, I trembled in front of four year olds. I wrote a song about recycling and endured a bout of diarrhea before singing to the second graders. Eventually, I wrote a song about women's history. Shaking like a leaf before a group of fifth graders, I sang about bravery and shared funny facts about famous women - women who turned ordinary lives upside down to fulfill their dreams.

After that presentation, a timid young child asked for my autograph. She said when she grew up she wanted to be like Florence Nightingale and *me*. In that moment, I saw how humor and music reached her. I pondered how the world might be different if we could all see past what makes us shake, and instead believe in possibility and greatness.

If fear of making a fool of myself was holding me back, perhaps it was holding others back. How could I possibly turn this terrifying stage fright and fear of embarrassment into something I could tolerate, let alone treasure?

First, I turned my suburban mom image Upside-

Down. I risked looking foolish and got "real." As I shared my own embarrassing moments, fears, and imperfections, other mothers and co-workers did the same. Soon we all found more humor in our daily car pools, work shifts, and weekly Weight Watchers meetings. We became kinder as we saw the authenticity and greatness in one another. I slowly began trusting myself.

Behind the eyes of the banker, boss, car repairman, and even the law enforcement officer are people just like us - in need of humor and acceptance. Can we flip frowns upside down, even in the tiniest day to day interactions? I believe we can.

I continued to make up funny songs and privately share true life tales about Lamaze class couples, my family, and my own domestic disasters. I was still waiting for some evidence the "wedding incident" had enriched my life when an opportunity to overcome stage fright boldly presented itself.

I was attending a conference in Wisconsin for burned out Lamaze teachers, when a stranger casually mentioned she liked my large pink earrings. This was her mistake. If you talk to me, I will follow you.

I proceeded to follow the poor women down the hotel corridor explaining how these particular earrings were made of sponges; hence they could be huge but not painful or heavy to wear. She walked a little faster as I elaborated on why I liked them, where I purchased them, and what I paid for them. Picking up my pace to match hers, I added, "I'm very resourceful. These earrings can be used to wipe down the microwave. They can be worn as a lovely fashion accessory, and they can be an effective contraceptive sponge!"

Needless to say, the woman walked even faster and we parted ways. Instead of listening to the next conference speaker, I spent the session chastising myself. "Deb," I scolded. "You are so inappropriate! You can't say contraception to a complete stranger. What in the world is wrong with you?"

Later, I submitted my evaluation form and thanked one of the event planners for providing such a lovely conference. She responded by asking what I thought would improve future conferences. After a pause, I suggested that adding music or humor might help nurses to focus on what we have in common and foster more networking.

"Great idea!" the woman replied. "Why don't YOU do that next year?" It was the perfect opportunity to say, "As a matter of fact, I have been writing a few songs and I will consider it." Instead, all I could utter was "Whoa. I just want to fill out the complaint form. I don't want to serve on any committee!" With that, she chuckled and invited me to meet someone in charge of area conferences.

Sure enough, I looked up to see the "earring lady" standing before me. "Oh yes, we met earlier," she said as she extended her hand and a smile. "Would you entertain us during the next conference?" she asked. I could have focused on the earring faux pas or fixated on the "wedding incident." Instead, I flipped potential stage fright (and cardiac arrest) Upside-Down and saw a unique opportunity. "Yes!" I answered bravely as I recited the ABC's of CPR under my breath.

Exactly a year later, I presented the first of what would become hundreds of songs and stories as a professional speaker and entertainer. I won't lie. At first I was terribly nervous, but every time the butterflies began, I flipped my emotions Upside-Down and embraced the opportunity to make a difference.

Even my travels turned Upside-Down. I could never have dreamed that one day I would be performing for nurses "Down Under" in Australia and New Zealand!

When I stand before an audience today, can I always be sure I won't freeze, transpose lyrics, or, worst of all, publicly spill my deepest thoughts in the middle of a song? Will I always have a witty retort for some jerk undermining my confidence?

Of course not, but when we have a plan to turn these moments Upside-Down, and focus on what is humorous, we consistently experience less fear, less pain, and less humiliation. When we are "real" and stay positive, our deepest desires surface and we see greatness and possibility. Even our most embarrassing moments can become treasured memories when taken with a big dose of laughter. So go ahead, "Make me laugh!"

# About the Author
## Deb Gauldin, RN, PMS

A professional speaker, author, recording artist, and entertainer, Deb uses original music, humor, and cartoons to replenish audiences who feel overextended and under appreciated. Specializing in healthcare morale and women's well being, her hilarious CDs, humor columns, and illustrations are used in wellness settings around the world. She is the past president of the National Speakers Association, Illinois Chapter and has served on the board of the Association for Applied and Therapeutic Humor. Though she has received numerous professional accolades and honors, Deb insists her best credentials are her stretchmarks and laughlines.

### Contact Information:
Deb Gauldin, RN
Deb Gauldin Productions
Phone: 800-682-2347
E-mail: deb@debgauldin.com
www.debgauldin.com

# Where There's a Will, There's a Way To Be Funny in the 21st Century

**By Randall Reeder**
**(With a Little Help from Will Rogers)**

Sometimes, I wish Will Rogers was still alive to make sense of the world today. I say this because I truly feel that was his gift.

Will took the big, confusing issues of the day and whittled them down to a few clear sentences. Then he dipped those sentences in humor, which usually took the sting out of the hard truths he had exposed. Once they were well-seasoned with wit, he hung them out to dry so everybody, from the U.S. Congress to the common man, could see.

Want to know the really amazing thing? Folks loved him for it.

Our country at war. High gas prices. The ruin that was once New Orleans. Hard truths, every one of them. Trust me, we could use Will around today. And I'm trying as hard as I can to "channel" the spirit of the great man so that we don't forget him. You and I may know who Will was and what he meant to our country, but our children may not. That's not something I want to see happen.

Whenever I thank the people who help me keep the wit, wisdom and legend of Will alive, I always include a man named Dale Minnick. Dale's first words to me when we met were "You've got to be Will Rogers."

Well, I wasn't, but he kept prodding me, even going as far as to say, "God put you here to remind people of the most admired man in the United States in the 20th century." I already looked and talked like him, so I studied Will, learned his history, took up his mannerisms and even tried to learn a couple of his rope tricks.

Then I started giving talks in Will's "voice." Big audiences, small audiences, it makes no difference to me, just like it would have made no difference to Will. I keep doing it because he was a man who could inspire a nation and because I believe his message is still relevant today.

Computers, cell phones, cable TV — you might say the world we live in is a far piece from the world Will once knew. But I believe something Will believed: The people sitting at their computers, talking on their cell phones (while paying too little mind to traffic!) and sitting up watching CNN are still very much the same as they ever were. And they're much more like each other than they might admit.

We need humor in much the same way as the people who listened and laughed at Will's humorous take on the American life did. Technology has evolved, but the average American? Not so much. He still has the same hopes and fears about life. The same insecurities, the same dreams for his children, and his children's children.

The more things change ....

## The Man Who Lassoed a Nation

Who was Will Rogers? Well, he was an American legend. Always the entertainer, he started in vaudeville in the early 1900s as a world-class rope trick artist and grew to be a multi-media giant. He had the ear of commoners and kings. In an all-too brief span from the early 1920s until his death in 1935, he was a movie star, weekly and daily newspaper columnist, radio commentator and professional speaker. He talked, and the world listened.

And more often than not, the world got a chuckle out of what he said.

Will's speaking style was casual, and he wrote the way he talked. He usually started slow, kinda feeling out his audience or the topic of the day. He used common, ordinary words at a time in our country's history when most prominent speakers prided themselves on being eloquent orators and most journalists wrote in stilted, proper English.

During the Great Depression, someone foolishly called Will to task over his grammar. "There's lots of folks that never say 'ain't' that ain't eatin'," he replied.

It's true that Will didn't receive much formal education, but you could never say that he wasn't an educated man. Will left school in the dead of night, got a job on a Texas ranch and never returned, but he never stopped learning.

"We're all ignorant, just on different subjects," he liked to say. "There's nothing as stupid as an educated man when you get him off the subject he was educated in." In all the years I've been repeating this bit of Will's wisdom, I've never yet had a woman disagree with it.

## I Never Met a Man I Didn't Like

Of course, if Will was saying that today, it would be "I never met a person I didn't like."

Joe Carter, the former director of the Will Rogers Museum in Claremore, Okla., told me he figures that when Will came up with that phrase, he was trying to make some big points about life and how to live it: How we shouldn't pre-judge someone before we really get to know them. How you shouldn't decide you won't like 'em based on what they look like or what you've heard or read about them.

But over the years, some people just mined it for its humor, and I think Will would have approved of the liberties folks have taken with "I never met a man I didn't like."

The legendary and seductive actress Mae West didn't change it at all when she used it. And not long ago, I heard 60 Minutes' Andy Rooney do a piece on store-front displays in which he decided, "I never met a mannequin I didn't like."

I don't know how he felt about mannequins, but Will liked people. He might criticize or poke fun at their decisions, but never the individual. His humor was never mean-spirited; something that never fails to inspire me. Can't really say that about some comedians you hear on cable TV today.

But the topics are still familiar. For instance, Will made a living joking about the people in Congress. "The thing about my jokes is they don't hurt anybody. You can say they're funny, or they're horrible, or they're good, whatever, but they don't do any harm.

"But with Congress, every time they make a joke it's a law … And every time they make a law, it's a joke." You would think Will would be mighty unpopular around the Capitol Building, which he called "the old joke factory." But in 1927, the National Press Club gave him the honorary title, "Congressman-at-Large," and nobody in Congress objected.

Like Will, I got a call to address several Congressmen, and no, it wasn't in the form of a subpoena. I spoke to the House of Representatives' Agriculture Committee and my expertise in the area of agriculture and Will's humor from the 1920s and 1930s served me well. They laughed whether I was poking fun at Republicans, Democrats or Texans. They did seem to enjoy it more when the joke was on the Senate or the President.

## All I Know Is What I Read in the Newspaper

Will was once asked, "Who writes your stuff and where do you get it?" His answer would be familiar to many of our most popular humorists working today, folks like Jay Leno or David Letterman: "The newspapers write it! I have found out two things: One is that the more up-to-date a subject is the more credit you are given for talking on it, even if you really haven't said anything very funny." Just stay up tonight and watch Leno or Letterman, and you'll see that our man Will knew what he was talking about.

And Will's second thing? That would be that, sometimes, the facts are funnier than any fiction you could come up with. "You can exaggerate and make it ridiculous, but it must have the plain facts in it. Then you will hear the audience say: 'Well, that's pretty near right.' ... Now rumor travels faster, but it don't stay put as long as truth," he said.

Right here, I'd like to point out that Will's humor was always clean. When he was on the road, Will was often invited to speak in church on Sunday morning. He'd use the same jokes and stories from Saturday night and get the same laughs. Maybe even more. I don't think many of today's comedians could say that. Try and imagine George Carlin or Chris Rock stepping into the preacher's spot. It's a mighty stretch, isn't it?

## Humor that keeps going and going and going

Will knew the value of a good quote. No doubt Leno, Letterman and Rock do, too. Comedians not only want to leave you laughing; they want you to repeat the best parts to your friends tomorrow. Then those folks will want to hear what you have to say and how you say it. Then, they'll tell their friends. Pretty soon you're turning down club dates and making plans for your next comedy special on HBO. Word of mouth, my friend, is still the best advertisement under the sun.

Pick up a book of Will's best quotations. Or visit my Web site, where I've collected more than a few for your enjoyment and education.

I'd like to leave you with some of my friend Will's words. As you can see, his humor is timeless and that leaves me plenty to work with today because Will was smart enough to joke about the things that never change: human nature and politics.

- "I'm not a member of any organized party. I'm a Democrat."
- "I'm able to tell the truth because I have never got mixed up in politics. The more you read and observe about this politics thing, you've got to admit that each party is worse than the other. The one that's out always looks the best."
- "There is only one redeeming thing about this whole election. It will be over at sundown, and let everybody pray that it's not a tie."

Will told about a "serious-looking young college

boy" who wanted to interview him about the business of being funny. The student had the questions written out, and Will talked him out of them, promising to send the answers along. Here's a highlight or two:

**Q:** Is the field of humor crowded?

**A:** "Only when Congress is in session."

**Q:** What talent is necessary? Must one be born with a funnybone in his head?

**A:** "It's not a talent, it's an affliction. If a funnybone is necessary, I would say that in the head is the place to have it. That's the least used of a humorist's equipment."

**Q:** "Is it profitable to read other Humorists?"

**A:** "Profitable but terribly discouraging."

If you ever have the time, it would be "profitable" to read all of the 31 questions and answers, which were published in *American Magazine*, September, 1929.

When people ask me how to be funny, I tell them everything I know about a simple-yet-great man named Will Rogers, and how he used common sense and his sense of the common man to teach a hurting nation that we must all laugh at ourselves before we can laugh with each other.

And I tip my hat to my old friend Will and repeat his best advice on the humorist's life:

"Get a few laughs, and do the best you can."

# About the Author

## Randall Reeder

Randall Reeder brings Will Rogers to life. Randall speaks as the American legend of the 1920's and 1930's who was a movie star, newspaper columnist, radio commentator and professional speaker. In his exciting program, Will Rogers Today, Randall helps people feel good about who they are and what they do. He uses the humor and wisdom of Will Rogers to address contemporary issues and entertain his audiences. Jim Rogers, son of Will Rogers, wrote of Randall's work, "I sure liked your speech and your writings. Great stuff."

### Contact information:

Randall Reeder
Will Rogers Today
4779 Baldwin Road
Hilliard, OH 43026
E-mail:will@willrogerstoday.com
www.willrogerstoday.com

# Parenting: Who's Raising Whom? In Search of That Elusive Parenting Manual

by Joe Gandolfo, M.A., LPC

My two boys test my patience, tear at my heart and don't listen to what I say or ask, and just flat out drive me bonkers! Oh, I love those two monkeys so much! I am a proud parent of two wonderfully beautiful kids who are nothing short of miracles and who bring joy to me every day. I will never forget the exact moments that Cole and Duncan were born. But they still drive me nuts.

## Let the Parenting Begin . . .

We brought our first son Cole home on Labor Day. *Labor* Day! Really! Home from the hospital and parked in the driveway, I could not get the baby basket to release from its base. Where is that manual? Tugging, pulling, and flabbergasted, I finally was able to get the safety seat free. *"Boy, this parenting stuff is hard,"* I thought. Little did I know.

Finally in the house, I set Cole's basket on the floor as my wife Tonya and I admired him from the couch. We looked at him; we smiled at each other. But in the instant my eyes linked back with the eyes of this little human being my excitement and exhaustion quickly turned to a contained panic.

*"WHAT DO YOU DO NOW . . . DAD?"* I thought. I realized in that moment that I had no clue what I was doing being a dad. Absolutely no idea.

I knew that old joke about how kids don't come with an instruction manual. And for the first time, I understood why it isn't really a joke. (Though, come to think of it, who was I kidding? I've never read the manual for *any* of the zillions of electronics we own; what made me think I'd read the kid manual? Still... I digress.)

We got lucky. During his first six months, Cole taught us how to parent him by letting us know what *he* needed. He couldn't talk, but his adorable coos and cries taught us all we needed to know to keep him happy. But after he taught us how to parent a newborn, he turned into a crawling baby. Just when we learned the game he changed the rules. But once again, he turned out to be a fine teacher.

Duncan, our second son, arrived five years later — again with no manual. (By this time you think I'd be over it and be an awesome natural dad. Nope... I wanted the instructions. Duncan didn't come with a manual either.)

But just like his big brother, Duncan proved to be a good teacher. I've finally come to understand that if we keep our sense of humor our kids will teach us as much as we teach them. We *never* get a manual. But if we keep a smile on our face there is a pretty good chance our kids will be the only guide we need. (Though, I still might need one for my fancy TV.)

# Fear and the Other Side

When the boys were a bit older we took them camping in a magnificent state park in Tennessee. It is a beautiful park, part of which features hiking trails connected by suspension bridges built over vast gorges. (In this case, "vast" means Indiana-Jones style, scare-the-breath-right-out-of-you-rickety bridges over deep—*really* deep— ravines.) As we approached a bridge about 100 yards long and suspended at least 150 feet into the air my oldest son took off across a bridge and called for the rest of us to follow.

I yelled out the typical parental concerns: "Be careful!" "Hang onto the rail!" "Walk slow!" "If the bridge breaks . . ." But in my mind I was yelling, "Son, get off that death trap because there is no way on God's Green Earth that I'm going to follow you! Now just be smart, turn around, and come back."

I wasn't a little scared. I was as scared as I have ever been. I was afraid for my son. And I was afraid for myself. But what is a parent going to do? If your kid crosses the bridge you have to follow, right? I started across, but was so afraid that I just wanted to go back. My son had happily crossed to the other side, totally unaware of my panic. I had a *choice* — to let my fear stop me or not. With each step, my fear increased, but I kept walking. When I reached the other side my son and I were both jubilant and euphoric. And I was relieved. We high-fived and laughed, then walked back across the bridge. I was amazed; my fear was gone.

What did I learn? I learned that I needed to be a lot more like my son. I needed to totally change my attitude when it comes to obstacles. There are times in our lives when we want to do something — be a better parent, improve our personal or work lives, go for our dreams, or cross a scary bridge — but fear can creep up inside of us, and we become unsure of ourselves. We chicken out and are doubtful that we can get to "the other side." Many of our fears are nothing more than irrational thinking and self-limiting beliefs. That bridge was perfectly safe; the real problem was in my head.

I was thinking about a million things as I crossed that bridge, and none of them were good. My son, on the other hand, was enjoying the view, savoring the movement of the cables, and generally loving the trip. Like Cole, I should have been thinking less and enjoying more.

Had I been on my own, I wouldn't have crossed the bridge. But who wants to look like a baby in front of a six year old? Cole just made a decision to go, and then he went. No second thoughts. No worries. No long internal discussions. He just went. And while he crossed, he enjoyed the journey. My son unknowingly offered me a lesson about fear, doubt, and self-limiting beliefs. I needed to be reminded that if you're busy enjoying the trip it's hard to be worked up about all the things that can go wrong. It was a life lesson, gift-wrapped and delivered by a first grader.

## Curiosity Did Not Kill The Cat

One day I was totally stressed out while working at home. Duncan was interrupting me with a question while I was on the phone. I told him that I was leaving a message in somebody's voice mailbox. "What's a voice mailbox?" Duncan asked. "Is it like the mailbox at the end of our driveway, but instead of holding letters, a voice mailbox holds recorded voice messages?" These were all good questions, but I really wanted him out of my office. I needed to get some stuff done.

"Where is the voice mailbox?" he persisted. Aaaagh! "A voice mailbox is inside computers at phone companies." Duncan walked to the back of the monitor, looked at it for a few moments, and said confidently, "I can see the voice mailbox!" Finally, I laughed. And I laughed hard.

Duncan and his adorable persistence, his unending curiosity, and his false understandings cracked me up. He reminded me that my calls weren't that important. That my work will get done.... later. He erased my stress and replaced it with laughter. And I'm supposed to be teaching him?

## The Game Of Life – Chutes and Ladders

Duncan came to me one morning and asked if I wanted to play. Being a part-time stay-at-home Dad mixed with the responsibility of growing a company, I was torn like an old faded pair of jeans. Only that faded old jeans are comfortable, and that for me taking time out on that busy day to "play" made me feel like I was wearing starched underwear.

"Yes, I want to play," part of me thought. "No! I have to work!" said the other part. Work will be there later; my kids are young now, so I said, "Ok, let's play."

He wanted to play CHUTES and LADDERS. "You've got to be kidding me – CHUTES and LADDERS? Come on little buddy how about poker?" CHUTES and LAD-DERS it was. (Partly because I couldn't find the poker chips.) In case it has been as long for you as it was for me, CHUTES and LADDERS is a horrible game. There is no skill, no strategy, and no thought required. Just spin the spinner, and move your smiley little person along the board. Avoid the "chutes" that drop you back. Hope for "ladders" that award you with shortcuts. I wasn't psyched, but I tried to be as happy as the people pieces looked.

We began to take turns and moving our pieces. I explained to him how to move his people piece along the rows towards the final square - THE ULTIMATE GOAL, the winning square with the blue ribbon and the gold numbers 1 – 0 – 0.

"To win the game, you have to get to this square," I told him. It was not long before he landed on a ladder, earning a shortcut and getting a bit closer to victory. I hit a slide and down I went, bummed not that I might lose but that this game might take forever. I needed to get back to work.

But when Duncan hit a slide he threw his hands above his head and hollered out a "Whoooooo". I looked at him puzzled. Didn't he understand that the slides are bad? We kept playing, taking turns moving our game pieces, climbing ladders with me repeatedly pointing out to Duncan the ULTIMATE GOAL. I kept thinking, "Win Duncan, Win!" I thought it was a great lesson about climbing the ladders of life. Climb. Work. Win. Besides, I wanted to get back to work.

Duncan had nearly won when he landed on the

space with the largest (read that, "worst") slide in the game. I expected tears, but again he threw up his arms and shouted another joyous "Whoooooo" I could not believe it! Not only was this game actually going to take another decade to finish, but Duncan was crazy enough to enjoy the slides most of all.

Again, it was the kid who taught the parent. I was focusing on the end goal and on who would win. Duncan just wanted to *play*.

The ladders of life are not the most important thing. He reminded me to enjoy the slides too. He reminded me to play, holler, laugh and enjoy — even when I'm going backwards. Duncan reminded me that it is often fun just to play, and that the end goal is secondary. He reminded me that as adults, we become obsessed with the *outcome,* when instead we should enjoy the *process*. Who knew a kid could be so deep?

Since that day I must confess that I've asked *him* to play CHUTES and LADDERS. (It is still a horrible game, but having a kid shout, "Whoooooo" while he loses is good for my heart.)

## Change and Mr. Put-It-Together

During the 2004 Christmas holidays, I transformed

into MR. PUT-IT-TOGETHER. I had many gifts to assemble for my boys, my wife, and myself. Some assembly required? No problem! I was off to get my new toolbox. (Hey, sometimes Dads get toys too.)

While I was busy assembling a trampoline, my oldest son Cole was playing nearby with a friend. At one point, to keep myself from going over the edge during a week of "being important," I began acting goofy. I was hooting, hollering, and singing – just plain trying to lighten up.

It wasn't long before my eight-year-young son came over to me and politely asked, "Dad, can you stop that? You're embarrassing me." Embarrassing? I had been silly like that for years. That was the first time my eight-year-old kid ever was critical of me.

But in that moment I realized my oldest was beginning a very important shift in his life. He no longer thought everything I did was *cool*. It was about time! (Now my wife had some company.) The way that he had related to me and needed me over these eight years was changing. I was still important to Cole, even though I sometimes "embarrass him." Cole was changing and growing as he should be, and I needed to shift and change the way I related to him and supported him.

Of course we need to change the way we relate to our kids as they grow. And if we listen, they will teach us what they need and when they need it.

Again, I was reminded that MR. PUT-IT- TOGETHER does more than put stuff together as his children grow: He also is needed to help his growing children put their lives together long after the bikes, Legos, trampolines, and such have been assembled.

## WHERE IS THAT PARENTING MANUAL?

Parenting is physically demanding when children are young, mentally demanding when they are older, and always emotionally charged because they have become a reflection of ourselves. Parenting is an adventure that demands an open mind. But even more so, it requires a sense of humor. And most of all, being a great parent means allowing your kids to teach *you*.

Oh how I yearn for the days when my biggest problem was a stuck car seat.

*WHERE IS THAT PARENTING MANUAL?*
*CHILDREN ARE THE MANUAL!*
*WHO IS RAISING WHOM?*

# About the Author

## Joe Gandolfo, M.A., LPC

Joe Gandolfo, "Americas DADvocate™", is on a mission to champion our greatest commodity in today's world – kids, young adults and college students, and to rally, strengthen and energize the adults – parents, educators, mental health professionals - who work with and care about the greatest commodity in the world.

Programs for kids, young adults and college students that are a smash hit! *What's Up With Parents These Days?™ A Guide To Raising Your Parents*, and, *Got H.I.P.?™ Hope, Inspiration and Perseverance Does A Life Great!*

Programs for parents, educators and mental health professionals: *A Daily Dose of Dad™*, *Parenting: Who Is Raising Who?™*, and, *Got H.I.P.?™ Hope, Inspiration, Perseverance and Working with Young People!*

His 17+ year professional background as a Licensed Professional Counselor, university teaching at Georgia Tech and a performance consultant to the Georgia Tech Athletic Association created the expertise. His personal journey as a kid, teen, college student, son, father of two boys and a "forever big kid at heart" guarantees his authenticity and fun!

A professional speaker, author and seminar leader who engages his audiences and gets them laughing, thinking, laughing, inspired and motivated!

## Contact Information:

Joe Gandolfo, M.A., LPC - Gandolfo Enterprises, Inc.
1000 Johnson Ferry Rd, B-200 Marietta, GA 30068
Phone: (678) 640-0000 • Fax: (678) 888-0384
E-mail: joe@JosephGandolfo.com
www.AmericasDADvocate.com

#  Laughter with a Lesson: Finding your Inner Joy

**By Carol Ann Small CLL, BSSP**

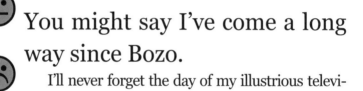

### Send in the Clowns.

You might say I've come a long way since Bozo.

I'll never forget the day of my illustrious television debut - at age 5 - on the "Bozo The Clown" show. My miniature heart skipped a beat as the host with the carroty colored hair and red nose invited me into the center ring. Here it was - my first opportunity to become an elementary school superstar! Bozo beckoned and I gave my all during the challenging ring toss competition. However, within seconds, my dreams of international celebrity were dashed. My toss tanked. I was sent back to my seat, feeling the complete agony of defeat. Nevertheless, I received an important message that day about bouncing back from life's little disappointments. From "Bozo" to the accomplished Humortarian that I am today, I have learned the true meaning of "Laughter With a Lesson."

In my Humor in the Workplace seminars, I stress how important it is to listen to your inner voice. If you're an unhappy stockbroker and you've always had intuitive inklings about starting your own cupcake factory, maybe it's time to pay attention to your innermost desires.

Of course, I'm speaking from personal experience. When I was working in higher education, my favorite part of the job was hamming it up during Emerson College's employee talent show. The applause I received after my performance reminded me of a treasured dream that I had put away.

## A Star Is Born: "Lights! Camera! ... Laundry?"

After my guest appearance opposite Bozo the Clown, I decided that the spotlight was definitely for me. My next public appearance — at age 7 — would be at a highly acclaimed underground theater. All right, it was in my family's basement. Nevertheless, I was determined to pursue my dreams of show-business glory.

Repeatedly emerging from my downstairs "42nd

Street," I would overwhelm my mother with relentless requests for props and backstage supplies: bedspreads, shoelaces, mascara, Elmer's glue.

Of course, red-velvet curtains were far beyond my five-and-dime budget, so this Doris Day wannabe had to get rather creative. Draped over my mother's clothesline was a powder-pink chenille bedspread coupled with a Zodiac beach towel — these borrowed treasures would serve as my colorful backdrop. Not exactly Radio City Music Hall, but now this leading lady was fully prepared for her grand entrance.

When I asked my mother if I could borrow her most expensive high heels, she became suspicious and inquired, "Carol Ann, what on earth are you doing down there? Opening up a Woolworth's?"

Nothing prepared me for Mom's grand inquisition, and something told me that maybe it wasn't the best time to confess that a major Broadway extravaganza — produced, directed, and starring Farragut Avenue's answer to Carol Burnett — was about to be staged in our cellar.

**Act One.** "The Carol Ann Small Show" debuts. As I launched into my spirited attempts at tap dancing to "Tip Toe Through The Tulips," in my mind I was defiantly tapping away all memories of my televised boo boo on Bozo.

**Act Two.** I'm seated at a slightly off-key, upright

piano and pouring out my eight-year-old heart to the tune of "You Make Me Feel Like A Natural Woman."

**Act Three.** For my grand finale, I dazzled the audience with my comedic monologue concerning the scandalous, real-life tragedy of learning that the promised prize for peddling the most Girl Scout cookies was . . . a box of Thin Mints.

The "curtain" closed and my faithful and ever encouraging piano teacher, Winnie Walsh, led the enthusiastic standing ovation. Little did I know that decades would fly by before I rediscovered the joy of making an audience laugh — and I mean spectators other than my childhood pal (and understudy) Cheryl Jean, my very generous mother and Happy, our family cat.

## A Case of Trial and Error

It took many years of creative trial-and-error before I realized that when we're not following our personal yellow-brick road to our heart's desire, we can end up feeling like life has dropped a house on us.

Classic example: Fresh out of high school — with my guidance counselor's less than sage advice to "marry well" still ringing in my ears — I attempted to become a court stenographer, a job that nearly pushed me over the edge.

I vividly remember my dad coming home one day and saying, "I'll tell you, honey, those court stenographers only work part time, and they make buckets of money!" I instantly thought: Job for me!

After six miserable months in the profession, I realized I had made a real doozy of a mistake. Sure, there were plenty of red flags along the way. For example, when I found myself in the third year of a two-year program that might have been a sign that something wasn't quite right.

It should have been obvious to me that I'd never win a Golden Globe for my court reporting. Part of the problem was that I was never one to sit quietly in the corner. I was a chatterbox, but judges tend to frown on their stenographers striking up animated conversations with the jurors, especially during a trial.

Instead, I sat there muted, all the time wanting to exclaim, "He's guilty! It's lunchtime. Anyone for chop suey?" Finally, one fateful day, I went out for the #6 special with egg roll, never to return to the halls of justice again.

## What I Did for Cash

In the '80s, while most people were wondering who shot J.R. on "Dallas," I couldn't help but wonder: who killed my dream? As I struggled to keep my head above water while attempting to finance my rusty 1973 Chevy Nova, I found myself putting my dreams aside. Staying one step ahead of the bill collector forced me to take many odd jobs, emphasis on the odd.

After struggling through a five-year medley of off-beat occupations and barely making ends meet by temping, delivering phone books, waitressing and working in a law firm, I had something resembling a checking account, but I was miserable and exhausted from the endless hours of overtime. Why couldn't I find a job where my penchant for punch lines and tendencies toward larger than life theatricality wouldn't necessarily result in time being docked from my paycheck?

Then at my lowest point, a friend dared me to enter a talent show lip-synching to a recording of "The Rose" by Bette Midler, who some people say I resemble. To my speechless surprise and thorough delight, I snagged first prize and received a rapturous standing ovation. It had been far too many years since that inspirational ovation in my basement. The dream was suddenly re-ignited, but there was still the nagging matter of that runaway Visa bill. Was there a job out there that would allow me to be funny, highly motivated and profitable all at the same time? No sooner had I asked myself this question than the phone rang. Another supportive colleague was on the line suggesting that I ring Emerson College, a Boston based communication school, and apply for a job there which would allow me to enroll and take two free classes a semester. To this overworked overachiever, that arrangement sounded better than a half price sale at Filene's Basement.

For the next several years as the alumni events planner at Emerson, I toiled 9-5 during the week, but my evenings and weekends were always reserved for my first love: keeping the big dream alive.

Destiny definitely smiled upon this late bloomer the day that I walked into one of my first classes at Emerson, a comedy workshop taught by the legendary Betty Hutton. After observing one of my earliest attempts at developing the first of my zany alter egos, Betty generously praised my attempts and encouraged me to make laughter my life's work. To have the beloved star of "Annie Get Your Gun" and "The Greatest Show On Earth" offer such life-altering advice was all this natural born ham needed to hear. This time, the message had come through loud and clear: It was time for me to take humor very seriously.

## Small's Steps to More Laughter

As I was in the midst of my last class at Emerson, my speech professor, Dr. Ken Crannell, suggested that I apply my flair for funny business to training seminars for the corporate sector. After all, who needed a good laugh more than executives and administrators wading through a sixteen-hour workday? The first time I addressed an audience as a professional speaker, I looked out into the crowd of seriously stressed staffers and knew that I had found my mission in life. From that day forward, I would be the very first CFO, Chief Funny Officer, saving the corporate world one laugh at a time.

One of my secrets to lightening up corporate culture is to introduce fun props into the work environment. I once had a speaking engagement at a bank where the vice-president, whom we shall call John Dough (not his actual name as my ATM fees are already high enough) was so taken with my Stress-Buster Humor Kits (containing stress ball, humor bookmark, smiley-faced giggle gavel, and bubble pen) that he got one for each of his employees. With one of my "laughter bags" (a portable laugh track) hidden in his pocket, "Mr. Dough" went from cubicle to cubicle handing out the kits while simultaneously activating the laughing bag. The laughter was contagious, and I was proud to report their morning assembly was anything but a "bored meeting."

When I personally need inspiration (and I don't have time to tap my troubles away), I read an uplifting biography of an illustrious go-getter and learn that even the greatest names in history have overcome seemingly insurmountable challenges during their journey to greatness...

One of my favorite success stories is about that imaginative innovator, Walt Disney. Mickey Mouse's mentor overcame many obstacles on his journey to the happiest place on earth, but he faced each challenge with the attitude that "It's kind of fun to do the impossible." Just think, Walt Disney bought some remote swampland in Florida and transformed it into a Magic Kingdom!

Of course, the moral of the story is: Sometimes, it's important for us to experience what we don't want in life in order for us to know what we do want.

Remember: the purpose of life is joy.

Or, as Joseph Campbell, said, "Follow your bliss!"

# About the Author

## Carol Ann Small, CLL, BSSP

From her television debut at age 5 on "Bozo the Clown" to her appearance on ABC's "Good Morning America," Carol Ann Small has been entertaining and educating audiences across the country for several decades.

Acclaimed as a nationally-recognized motivational humorist and a stress management consultant, Carol Ann specializes in customized presentations which blend wisdom and laughter. Her comical ad-libs during audience participation have brought the house down.

From corporations to national conventions, organizations intent on boosting morale, motivating staffers or de-stressing employees have turned to Carol Ann for her unique perspective on the benefits of laughter and finding humor in the workplace and everyday life.

Carol Ann's clients include: Dunkin' Donuts, AVON, Bank of America, Harvard Pilgrim Health Care, Scholastic, Comcast, Aetna, Hewlett-Packard, Hilton, Tyco Healthcare, and the U.S. District Court.

Carol Ann has also enjoyed performing as a comedienne at Emerson's Majestic Theatre, Panache NYC and Boston's Comedy Connection.

Her name may be "Small" but her presence is larger than life!

## Contact Information:

Carol Ann Small, CLL, BSSP
LAUGHTER WITH A LESSON
Melrose, MA (Boston Area)
Phone: (781) 662-2078
Email: CarolAnn@Smallspeak.com
www. CarolAnnSmall.com

# Humor and Hurricanes.
# Humor Lessons In Tragedy and Loss

**An interview with**
**Bruce S. Wilkinson, CSP**

***Editor's Note:*** *During the creation of this book, Bruce Wilkinson and his family had their lives up-rooted by Hurricanes Katrina and Rita. A resident of New Orleans, Bruce and his family evacuated with thousands of other Louisianans. He lived for over a month in Alexandria, LA with family, not knowing how much he lost, but assuming that his home and office were destroyed.*

*To complicate matters, Bruce's grown daughter was pregnant and experienced several false labors, eventually giving birth to a premature little girl named Bella, who remained hospitalized for some time. Then Bruce's daughter went back into the hospital for complications resulting from the birth.*

*Bruce agreed with us that his experiences with this tragedy would make a great chapter, especially from his viewpoint of a humorist. This interview took place on the first day he was allowed back into*

*New Orleans. Bruce's daughter and granddaughter are*
*out of the hospital and are doing great. And to his surprise*
*and delight, his house and office are damaged, but largely*
*escaped the worst of it and unlike thousands of others are*
*salvageable.*

**Humor Us:**   Bruce, we're so glad you are safe and dry,
and that your family is well and out of the hospital. You've
been through a very tough time.

**BW:** Yes, we all have, but you won't hear any complaints
from me.

**Humor Us:** What do you mean?

**BW:**   What I mean is that yes, I was right in the middle of
America's largest natural disaster, ever. And yes, my family and friends have been through some health struggles,
to say the least. But as I sit here talking to you, Brad, I
know I'm a lucky man. My family is safe, I can rebuild and
in some ways I'm a better person for having experienced
Katrina.  I am more able to enjoy the little things in life,
and I am better able to appreciate all of my blessings.

**Humor Us:**   I have no trouble believing that you are a
positive guy now that the worst of it is behind you. But tell

us how it was for you during the darkest times. You're a professional humorist, and a professional speaker who, among other things, speaks to your audiences about leadership, character and positive attitudes. But there must have been times when you were unable to practice what you preach. When you were hopeless, sad, depressed, and...

**BW:** And alive! I was still alive. Brad, I'm telling you, I have a strong commitment to keeping a positive attitude, and that didn't change during the disaster.

**Humor Us:** Can you tell me how you did it? How *could* you have a good attitude when times were so hard?

**BW:** When you think and act positive, it feeds on itself and others can feed off it. My friends and family have always looked to me as the motivational speaker, the comedian, and the joker. So when we were faced with this evacuation, with this loss, and with what was for so many a sense of hopelessness, I tried to maintain my role. I was upbeat in part because the people around me expected me to be upbeat. You know what it's like, Brad. You're a humorist as well. You can't even go to the bathroom in a bad mood because an audience member will say, "Why aren't you smiling?" I'll say, "I'm going to the bathroom."

But they want us to smile anyway — they expect us to always bring our "A" game. I've always been an upbeat person with a very positive attitude. It's hard for me to be depressed because I have a long track record of *not* being unhappy. When our situation became very depressing and seemingly hopeless, it didn't pull me down because it was actually easier and more natural for me to stay positive. I'm just a guy who helped himself by helping others; a guy who found laughter in making others laugh. I was generally upbeat before Katrina and Rita, (or as I like to call them together, "Kat-rita,") and so I was generally upbeat after the hurricanes.

**Humor Us:**  You're saying that the decisions and choices you've made about the kind of person you want to be *before* the tragedy just carried through both during and after Kat-rina?

**BW:** Yes. Let me expand. I saw people in that disaster separate themselves into three sense-of-humor types.

First, there were the people who have *always* had a sense of humor, and kept that sense of humor throughout the disaster and evacuation. I don't mean every minute – but most of the time. These are the same people who had hope when there was no hope, and were able to give others hope. These are the people who, both before, during and *after* the storm, were able to smile, laugh at themselves, and most importantly share that sense of lightheartedness with others. I'm not saying that this group was *always* running about with a smile on their face, but for the most part, this group was able to stay optimistic and share that positivism.

The second group was probably negative, mad, angry and unhappy before Katrina hit, and stayed that way throughout. Nothing was going to change these people's attitude. Nothing could ever make it better for them and they always blamed someone else for both what has happened to them and what will happen to them. Food wasn't hot food, they had t.v., but no cable. If you sent them a helicopter to save their lives, they complained that it came too late. If you gave them a cot, they'd complain about not having a bed. If you gave them $2000 for groceries they'd complain that they didn't get $5000. These people were the loudest complainers about FEMA, the Red Cross/government response, and perceived racism.

The last and largest group was the one in the middle. They weren't leading the way to laughter, but they would allow themselves to be led into good humor. With encouragement and a little inspiration, these folks had some hope and humor. They could be won over. Maybe they weren't the type to *make* jokes, but they could laugh at them and gravitate towards those who laughed as well.

These groups existed before, during and after the storms. The hurricanes and flooding didn't change their personalities at all, it just amplified them. It's the same thing in the workplace with people who are different. They started out as different kids and now they are different adults.

**Humor Us:**   Were upbeat and positive people able to make a difference?

**BW:**  You bet, and to a greater extent than I had imagined. One of the biggest lessons for me is that we as individuals can make a far greater impact on others than I thought possible. People who could smile, stay positive, make others laugh, tell stories — whatever — were in big demand because they were genuinely needed. And if you could do any of those things *and* could play a guitar, then you were Superman!

**Humor Us:**  Are you serious?  A guitar?

**BW:**  Yes. There was little escape from our problems. Blockbuster was closed. (*Bruce laughs.*)   And of course, there was no electricity. Therefore, no cable. People needed any sort of escape and human connection they could get. So those who had any communication or entertainment skills really were in a position to help. If you could tell stories to the children, play a harmonica, sing, make people laugh, — do anything — it helped more than you could imagine.

For example, because I was a reserve police officer in the emergency rescue division for over two decades, I went back into New Orleans about a week after the hurricane to see if I could help. There were a variety of rescue workers and I mixed in with them. And as we were doing our best to lend a hand, we came upon three jazz musicians standing in a boat, on dry land playing Dixieland. They were playing, singing and doing what New Orleans is famous for: throwing out Mardi Gras beads and asking for tips.

When our crowd heard the music our moods changed instantly. Suddenly there was singing and laughter where there had been none. We lost our sense of desperation and hopelessness. Those musicians gave us back our sense of humor and reminded us of our fun-loving culture – it gave us hope!

Not only were they giving us the gift of humor; not only did they give us a mental break from this horrible rescue job; I'm convinced that they *needed* to help. They helped themselves by giving us the gift of their music. By raising our spirits they raised their own spirits. They needed to contribute by doing what they did best before the disaster because that's who they are.

**Humor Us:**   Music, laughter and stories. It seems like such a simple thing.

**BW:** Exactly, but it was huge. It reinforced what I've always believed about the power of a positive attitude, the effectiveness of a well-placed, appropriate joke, and the influence of a lighthearted frame of mind. It can make a huge difference... and it does. For example, let me tell you about our attempt to rent a movie.

I was in a video store in Alexandria (after the power was back on but well before we were allowed to go back to New Orleans) trying to rent a movie. The store was crowded with many other evacuees with the same idea.

Well, of course we had no local address and the one we left wasn't looking too good either. We all had credit cards and drivers' licenses, but none of us had local documented addresses. We joked that our address was currently, "The Mississippi River." The store's rules required the renter's regular address, and the local lady behind the counter was going to stick with procedure. Tempers started to flare because we were all going to be denied. No address. No movies. No escape.

I kind of took over and, in a lighter tone, explained that all of us needed a break. We had money. We had identification. But — in case she might have missed it on the news

— our houses were ... well...kinda missing. I joked that we didn't really want to steal the movies as we didn't even have any players to put them in. (We of course were *borrowing* our hosts' players.) I asked her to be a little more flexible like we've had to be.

In the end we all left with movies; we all left with a 90 minute ticket to escape. It was no big deal, but by just bringing a sense of lightheartedness and a smile we were able to make a difference and it was a win-win for everyone – humor is a great crowd control weapon.

Here's another example, Brad. My son-in-law and I decided to apply for a food-stamp-like program for hurricane victims called the Louisiana Purchase. It was basically a handout; a credit card to be used for food, worth between $200 - $500 based on need. Now I'm a proud man. I've had a job since I was 16; it took 12 years of night school college courses to get where I am today. I've never asked for help. Ever.

But I needed this card. Not just for me, but I needed it to help the family that was taking us in by using the card to replace the food they had been providing. And as hard as it was for me to ask for help, it was even harder for my son-in-law. He is a good man; a proud, hardworking country boy. He had never asked for help either and going into this office to fill out the forms was hard on him because he was born and raised here. When we pulled up to the office, he told me he didn't feel comfortable asking for help. Suppose he saw some government workers who knew him and his family?

Both of our families needed some help. We had evacuated New Orleans and assumed we had lost everything. I suggested that he just "accompany" me. "Come in and you can be this old guy's driver. You're just my helper because you are from here and I'm lost." He liked that. "Yeah, Mr. Bruce. That works. We can do that." So he came in as my helper. And in the end, he saw what I saw: that the place was filled with other hard-working folks who just needed some temporary assistance. We *both* ended up leaving — five hours later — with the food cards.

**Humor Us:** Humor helped him feel at ease. Is that what you're saying?

**BW:** Yes. A little humor and a different perspective. That's what humorists do. But the wonderful part is that by making him feel comfortable, I ended up making myself more comfortable. As I said, I'm a proud man too and I've never asked for help. I wasn't excited about that place either. But by helping him out I was helping myself as well.

**Humor Us:** Let me change the subject a bit. You've told me that while you were away from New Orleans, you had to travel to one of your speeches. What was that like to leave your family during such difficult times?

**BW:** It was especially difficult because I was leaving my pregnant daughter behind. She had already gone through a couple false, pre-term labors, and I didn't want to leave but I had a commitment.

I was in Indiana preparing to go on stage for my keynote. The client had already started to introduce me when I answered my cell phone and found out that they were rushing my daughter to the hospital; that she had gone into premature labor. Pretty upsetting to say the least.

But I went out on stage and did the program. I told my audience about my house and office that probably were lost, and about my daughter who was at that very moment going into premature labor. I delivered my program about teamwork, positive attitudes and keeping hope alive. I am proud that when I am on stage I am able to really be there for that particular audience, and this date was no different. I was on stage for them, and I was able to stay focused on them.

And you know what?

It might have been helpful to them. But was helpful for me too. It was beneficial for me to feel useful just like the three musicians in the boat. It was good for me to keep my commitment and to think of others before myself. It also helped me to stay optimistic by reminding others of the importance of staying positive. I needed to be needed and to make a difference. By putting that audience before me, it not only gave me a break from a negative environment but their caring helped me to heal and feel hopeful myself.

After the program, a woman from the audience gave me her card with instructions to "read the back later." I didn't think much of it at the time and went to the airport focusing on what I was returning to. But later, as I was waiting for my plane, two amazing things happened.

First, I read the card. It said, "Have you ever heard the phrase, 'I was having a bad day, and this helped?' Well, I was having a bad CAREER, but I feel better now. Thanks so very much." Can you imagine? I have that card in my wallet right now.

And then, just seconds later, my client calls to tell me that after I left they passed a Subway sandwich bag around — not even a basket or a hat, but a fast food bag! — and that audience donated over $4,000 to be given to the Red Cross for the Katrina victims. I just cried. Bawled like a baby. (I found out later that they raised *another* $14,000!)

Do you see my point? I *had* to go to that program, partly because I am a man who believes in keeping my commitments. But equally important, by doing that job and focusing on others we created some magic. Had I *not* gone to Indiana, had I elected to stay with my family, I still would not have been able to physically help my daughter. She was fine and had others to help her; I told her, "I'm the grandfather – not the father!" And had I stayed home, that woman in my audience wouldn't have been given whatever it was she needed. And of course they wouldn't have collected $18,000 for the Red Cross.

**Humor Us:** So what happened when you got home?

**BW:** Well, as you can imagine, it took quite some time to get back to Alexandria because all of the flights had to be funneled into Baton Rouge and most of those seats were being taken by relief workers. My daughter started to go into serious labor on the night of 9/11 and she told the doctor that Bella Marie was not going to have a birthday on the same day as the 9/11 attack on New York. Well, she held on until the morning of 9/12 but she was born weeks premature and had some lung and heart problems. It pained me to see my little girl's little girl with all of those tubes and I.V.'s in her – so sometimes at night I would go into the intensive care unit and sing to her and some of the other newborn evacuated infants with challenges. It was sad Brad. There was even one evacuated newborn that was addicted to crack cocaine at birth. Anyway, I would make up some goofy song lyrics that had nothing to do with the original music and the nurses thought that I was the goofiest grandfather that they had ever seen. I even apologized for the disruptions but one of them told me to keep it up and that they too needed to smile and laugh because it helped keep their minds off of some of the sadness around them. Later that night, one of them even joined me in a duet of the Righteous Brothers' "You've Lost That Loving Feeling" (a version that will never be heard by the public). Once again Brad, helping them helped me too!

**Humor Us:** So help us sum this up, Bruce. What is the lesson in this disaster? What role can humor, lightheartedness and a positive attitude play in the presence of tragedy, pain, hopelessness and loss?

**BW:** I learned that there is always hope. And humorous hope is even better. I learned that the good in people far outweighs the bad. Over and over again I saw everyday people acting like heroes and helping others. More people want to do good than do harm, and we need to find these people and keep them in our lives for as long as possible.

I learned that no matter how hard things are now and no matter how bad things get, it can always be worse. You can't be worried about water damage and lost income when you see a person in a wheel chair on the sidewalk covered with a cloth — because they are dead. I have most of my family and friends. And my love of life. I'm a lucky man now and forever.

But most of all, I learned that helping others, doing the right thing, being positive, optimistic and sharing a smile, a laugh, and a lighthearted attitude comes back to you every time. I'm telling you, you get more out of it than you are giving. When you are giving from your heart it can change the world around you. By helping others to heal you are able to heal yourself. We can, with our positive attitudes, our light-heartedness, and our senses of humor make things better for others and for ourselves. On the way into the rescue area I saw a sign on the front porch of a house that was put there to prevent looting. It read, "I'm an angry man with a gun, ugly wife, a mean dog and a claw hammer –make my day!" A few days later when I left the sign read, "Still armed and angry, wife has gone but the dog is still mean and hungry. Come on in." This poor man lost everything — but his sense of humor.

Let me share a little joke that I told that audience in Indiana during the evacuation. I opened up my keynote by saying, "My name is Bruce Wilkinson and I come from the great city of New Orleans, LA, where our unofficial motto used to be, 'If you can't have fun here – it's your fault." Now our motto is, 'Hey, you got a boat?'"

# About the Author
## Bruce S. Wilkinson, CSP

Bruce S. Wilkinson, CSP is a professional leadership, communication and customer service speaker, trainer, author and implementation specialist who reinforces personalized messages with humor, passion, enthusiasm and authenticity. His mission is to help organizations translate their corporate culture into a workplace climate that inspires excellence. Bruce recently completed two three-year terms as an elected member of the Board of Directors of the National Speakers Association and is one of fewer than 650 people worldwide to earn the prestigious Certified Speaking Professional (CSP) designation. He also recently retired after twenty-two years of volunteer service as a post certified reserve police officer with the Jefferson Parish Sheriff's Office, where he worked in patrol, emergency rescue and as a member on the police academy staff.

As President and Chief Leadership Officer of Workplace Consultants, Inc. and Wilkinson Seminars and Presentations, he has presented in all 50 states, delivering enthusiastic keynotes and training programs for twenty years to clients such as Sara Lee, Six Flags, Xerox, Hallmark Cards, State Farm Insurance, Kellogg's, T.G.I. Friday's, the Department of Defense, NASA and two of his all-time favorites – Miller Brewing & Jack Daniel's.

## Contact Information:
Bruce S. Wilkinson, CSP - Workplace Consultants, Inc.
1799 Stumpf Blvd., Bldg 3, Ste 6B • Gretna, LA 70056
Phone: (504) 368-2994 • Fax: (504) 368-0993
E-mail: SpeakPoint@aol.com
www.WilkinsonSpeaker.com

# humor Us Some More!

### Still Craving More?

Lookin' for free articles, jokes, gags and humor ideas? Need to buy some hilarious props, toys and gags to spice up your workplace? Do you need a coach to help you with your sense of humor your presentations? Are you in the market for more books, audios, or videos about humor and laughter?

### What can you do? Where can you go?

Put this book down right now and visit ALL of the authors' websites. They are chock-full of resources—and other funny stuff—you can use to add humor to your life. Stuff that will make you smile; things that will make you laugh.

(You can even buy more copies of this book!)

**Mike Rayburn**
Take Out Anything That's Not Funny ...
The Habit of Champions

**Contact Information:**
Mike Rayburn
Quantum Talent
Phone: (843) 839-1668
www.mikerayburn.com

**Bill Stainton**
Eureka! Unlock Your Natural
Creativity with Humor

**Contact Information:**
Bill Stainton
Ovation Consulting Group, Inc.
Phone: 888-5BEATLE (523-2853)
www.OvationConsulting.com

**Steve Spangler, CSP**
Flying Potatoes and Exploding Soda:
The Secret to Creating Unforgettable
Learning Experiences

**Contact Information:**
Steve Spangler
Steve Spangler Science
Phone: (800) 223-9080
www.SteveSpanglerScience.com

### Patt Schwab Ph.D., CSP
How to Get More Humor In Your Life Without Being Clown

**Contact Information:**
Patt Schwab, Ph.D., CSP
FUNdamentally Speaking
Seattle, WA
Phone: 206-525-1031
Patt@FUNdamentallySpeaking.com

### Brad Montgomery, CSP
Humor Is ~~Not~~ A Business Word

**Contact Information:**
Brad Montgomery, CSP
Brad Montgomery Productions, Inc
Denver, CO
Phone: (800) 624-4280
www.BradMontgomery.com

### Jana Stanfield, CSP
Present Life Lessons From a Stand-Up Comedy Career

**Contact Information:**
Jana Stanfield
Keynote Concerts, Inc. • Nashville, TN
Phone: (888) 530-5262
Email: Business@JanaStanfield.com
www.JanaStanfield.com

**Michael C. Anthony, C.Ht.**
Creating Moments of Laughter

**Contact Information:**
Michael C. Anthony, C.Ht
Quantum Talent
Phone: (843) 839-1668
www.michaelcanthony.com

**Patty Wooten, RN, BSN**
Good Health IS a Laughing Matter

**Contact Information:**
Patty Wooten, RN, BSN
Phone: (888) 550-5378
Email pwooten@JestHealth.com
www.JestHealth.com

**Anne Barab**
Purple Hair, Or How To Laugh
About the Tough Stuff

**Contact Information:**
Anne Barab
Barab Associates, Inc.
Dallas, Texas
Phone: (877) 349-2777
www.AnneBarab.com

### Craig Zablocki
Fear of Having Fun

**Contact Information:**
Craig Zablocki
634 Marion St.
Denver, CO 80218
Phone: (303) 830-7996
Fax: (303) 830-0194
craig@PositivelyHumor.com
www.PositivelyHumor.com

### Tim & Kris O'Shea
The Experience of a Lifetime (Humor and Marriage)

**Contact Information:**
Tim and Kris O'Shea
Experience Productions
Westminster, CO
Phone: 303-371-2849
www.ExperienceProductions.net

### Brad Barton
Got Magic? Don't pull disasters out of thin air; use your powers to see what's really there

**Contact Information:**
Brad Barton
Brad Barton Communications, Inc.
Ogden, UT
Phone: (888) GOT-MAGIC
(468-6244)
Brad@BradBartonSpeaks.com
www.BradBartonSpeaks.com

### Michael Aronin
Humor in Action

**Contact Information:**
Rising Above
152 Langdon Farm Cr.
Odenton, MD 21113
Phone: (410) 672-2565
www.michaelaronin.com

### Deb Gauldin, RN, PMS
The Upside of Upside-Down Using
Humor to Turn Embarrassing
Moments into Treasured Memories

**Contact Information:**
Deb Gauldin, RN
Deb Gauldin Productions
Phone: 800-682-2347
E-mail: deb@debgauldin.com
www.debgauldin.com

### Randall Reeder
Where There's A Will, There's a Way
to Be Funny in the 21st Century - Will
Rogers and Today's Humor

**Contact Information:**
Randall Reeder
Will Rogers Today
4779 Baldwin Road
Hilliard, OH 43026
E-mail:will@willrogerstoday.com
www.willrogerstoday.com

### Joe Gandolfo, M.A., LPC

Who is Parenting Whom? In Search of That Elusive Parenting Manual

**Contact Information:**
Joe Gandolfo, M.A., LPC
Gandolfo Enterprises, Inc.
Phone: (678) 640-0000
Fax: (678) 888-0384
www.JosephGandolfo.com

### Carol Ann Small, CLL, BSSP

Take This Job And Love it!
Send in the Clowns and
You'll Find Your Inner Joy

**Contact Information:**
Carol Ann Small, CLL, BSSP
LAUGHTER WITH A LESSON
Melrose, MA   (Boston Area)
Phone:   (781) 662-2078
Email: CarolAnn@Smallspeak.com
www. CarolAnnSmall.com

### Bruce Wilkinson, CSP

Humor and Hurricanes.
Humor Lessons In Tragedy and Loss

**Contact Information:**
Bruce S. Wilkinson, CSP
Workplace Consultants, Inc.
1799 Stumpf Blvd., Bldg 3, Ste 6B
Gretna, LA  70056
Phone: (504) 368-2994
Fax: (504) 368-0993
E-mail: SpeakPoint@aol.com
www.WilkinsonSpeaker.com

# Need Someone to Come to You and Make Your Group Laugh?

Does your company have a meeting? An annual event? Do you attend a convention that could benefit from one of these very funny motivational speakers? Please contact the authors to learn about how they can help you to add the power of laughter to your convention, meeting, or program.

**Michael C. Anthony, C.Ht.** .................. www.MichaelCAnthony.com

**Michael Aronin** .......................................... www.MichaelAronin.com

**Anne Barab** .......................................................... www.AnneBarab.com

**Brad Barton** .............................................. www.BradBartonSpeaks.com

**Joe Gandolfo, M.A., LPC** ......................... www.AmericasDadvocate.com

**Deb Gauldin, RN, PMS** .................................... www.DebGauldin.com

**Brad Montgomery, CSP** .............................. www.BradMontgomery.com

**Tim and Kris O'Shea** ...................... www.ExperienceProductions.net

**Mike Rayburn** ................................................ www.MikeRayburn.com

**Randall Reeder** ........................................ www.WillRogersToday.com

**Patt Schwab Ph.D., CSP** ............www.FUNdamentallySpeaking.com

**Carol Ann Small, CLL, BSSP** ........................www.CarolAnnSmall.com

**Steve Spangler, CSP** ........................ www.SteveSpanglerScience.com

**Bill Stainton** ............................................ www.OvationConsulting.com

**Jana Stanfield, CSP** ....................................... www.JanaStanfield.com

**Bruce S. Wilkinson, CSP**............................. www.WilkinsonSpeaker.com

**Patty Wooten, RN, BSN** ..........................................www.JestHealth.com

**Craig J. Zablocki** ................................................ www.PositivelyHumor.com